S0-APP-329

NEW YORK'S
GREATEST
THOROUGHBREDS

NEW YORK'S
GREATEST
THOROUGHBREDS

A Contemporary History

ALLAN CARTER

THE
History
PRESS

Published by The History Press
Charleston, SC
www.historypress.com

Copyright © 2022 by Robert Allan Carter
All rights reserved

First published 2022

Manufactured in the United States

ISBN 9781467149211

Library of Congress Control Number: 2022935414

Notice: The information in this book is true and complete to the best of our knowledge. It is offered without guarantee on the part of the author or The History Press. The author and The History Press disclaim all liability in connection with the use of this book.

All rights reserved. No part of this book may be reproduced or transmitted in any form whatsoever without prior written permission from the publisher except in the case of brief quotations embodied in critical articles and reviews.

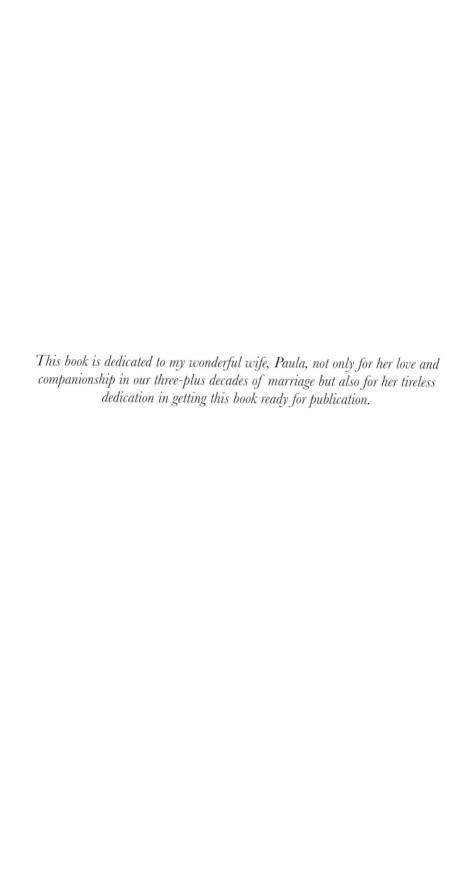

This book is dedicated to my wonderful wife, Paula, not only for her love and companionship in our three-plus decades of marriage but also for her tireless dedication in getting this book ready for publication.

R. Allan Carter, my dear husband, passed away on April 10, 2022. This book you are reading will be his last contribution to Thoroughbred racing scholarship. His passing is difficult to accept, as he was a young eighty-one, still enthralled with the Saratoga Race Course and worldwide racing. One of the last trips he took was to Japan with his Army friends, and while there, they visited some local stables. He was childlike in his excitement as he described the beautiful facility and its future impact on the sport.

Allan fell in love with racing and remained faithful to this love until he left the world. He always was seeking to learn more and, upon finding it, wanted to share what his research uncovered. When the National Museum of Racing and Hall of Fame offered him the position as its official historian, he felt he had landed his dream job. I know racing scholars and enthusiasts who loved the sport as much as he did will miss his quick mind and diligent efforts to find the facts he and others were searching for. What turned out to be Allan's last endeavor was to show the worth of New York–breds. This is why he wrote New York's Greatest Thoroughbreds—*to document the history of the many successful modern New York–bred horses. It is my hope that this work will finally show the racing community that Thoroughbred horses born in the Empire State can succeed anywhere in the world.*

It is also my wish that the Thoroughbred racing community and public will remember for years to come Robert Allan Carter's scholarly contributions to Thoroughbred racing and his generous and caring spirit.

His loving wife,
Paula Curtis-Carter

CONTENTS

FOREWORD

Racing historian Allan Carter, who served in that capacity for sixteen years at the National Museum of Racing and Hall of Fame in Saratoga Springs, New York, has written an authoritative and historically important work that complements the long history of Thoroughbred racing and breeding in New York State.

Saratoga Race Course is the oldest existing Thoroughbred track in the United States. Its first race meeting, of just four days, was conducted in the summer of 1863 on a trotting track across from what is today the main entrance of Saratoga Race Course. Racing moved across the street to its present location in 1864, and the Travers Stakes, which is the oldest stakes race for 3-year-olds in the United States, was inaugurated at the new track that year.

The great New York–bred filly Ruthless, owned by turf patron Francis Morris, won the fourth edition of the Travers in 1867, a year in which she also captured the inaugural running of the Belmont Stakes at Jerome Park, which opened in 1866. Mr. Morris was breeding top Thoroughbreds in Westchester County, setting a high bar for New York–breds of the twentieth and twenty-first centuries. Future generations of New York–breds would scale that bar, earning national championships and winning the most important stakes races at major racing centers across the United States.

The state itself committed to the benefits of Thoroughbred racing with the creation of the New York State Breeding and Development Fund in 1973. Commonly referred to as "the Fund," the program consisted of monetary incentives to those who invested in New York farmland with the purpose of Thoroughbred breeding.

The idea, in addition to recovering and preserving green space, was to encourage the raising and racing of horses born in New York State. The Fund stands as a remarkable example of public and private cooperation and has yielded Thoroughbreds that can compete with those born elsewhere in the United States.

Carter gives the readers their careers in this work. Some of the horses he wrote about—such as Funny Cide, Fleet Indian, La Verdad and Dayatthespa—earned Eclipse Awards as national champions in their respective divisions. Fio Rito did not win a national championship, but his dramatic upset in the prestigious Whitney Handicap at Saratoga Race Course in 1981, which followed his breaking through the gate before the start, made racing fans everywhere pay attention to the horses being bred in New York State.

A good horse, maybe a great horse, can come from anywhere, and in this book, Allan Carter tells us of the careers of the good ones from the Empire State.

—MICHAEL VEITCH, Historian
National Museum of Racing and Hall of Fame

ACKNOWLEDGEMENTS

No book is the product of one person, and in this case, there was a host of people who helped in making this one a reality. Although I have worked with computers for more than thirty-five years, they still remain a mystery, and my wife, Paula, has always been there to make the unfathomable fathomable, and for that I will always be in her debt.

I experienced many difficulties in getting photos for this project because of the pandemic, but Michele ("one L") Williams was able to delve into her well-organized collection to provide me with the insert photos I needed. Without her help, my book would have been less complete. Stephanie Luce and Vicki Reisman of the National Museum of Racing and Hall of Fame were also able to help me in this area. Stephanie Cooley from the Dubai Racing Club and Takayumi Ui from the Japan Racing Association were helpful in getting important insert photos along with the necessary permissions to use them.

Mike Veitch, who succeeded me as the historian at the National Museum of Racing and Hall of Fame and knows more about the history of New York–breds than anyone on the planet, proofed my book and found errors that only someone with his knowledge could have found.

Mike McGuire and Shawn Purcell of the New York State Library were able to provide me with the necessary materials I needed to explain the New York State Thoroughbred Breeding and Development Law.

Banks Smither of The History Press could not have been more helpful in explaining the process in getting the book to print and was also able to explain the intricacies of indexing to my wife, as well as supporting me in more mundane matters.

Special thanks go to my stepson Patrick Curtis for reconstructing my trusty computer after it crashed. I do not think I could have worked with any other computer.

INTRODUCTION

In 1973, the New York State legislature passed L.1973 Chapter 346, which included a section establishing a Thoroughbred Breeding and Development Fund. It provided money for New York Racing Association (NYRA) tracks (i.e., Aqueduct, Saratoga and Belmont, as well as Finger Lakes Race Track) to run races for New York–breds for more lucrative purses that had hitherto been paid. In addition, extra money would be paid to the owner of any New York–bred who finished first, second or third in an open stakes race. The money for the Fund would come from prescribed percentages of the wagering pools for all Thoroughbred races conducted in the state. It also defined New York–breds as foals that had been sired by registered New York sires and whose dams were registered New York broodmares. It was hoped that this would give New York breeders an incentive to produce more foals, as well as encourage more breeders to start up farms in the state.

When one looks for who was responsible for suggesting and drawing up the legislation in order to establish legislative intent, there is no such information to be found. The most likely source seemed to be the Governor's Commission on the Future of Horse Racing in New York State, but the commission's 160-page "Final Report," issued in 1973, made no mention of the breeding aspect of the sport. The Governor's Bill Jacket[1] for the law included few memoranda, none of which mentioned breeding.

Although the 1973 law resulted in an improvement in the state's breeding program, by 1994 there was evidence of another regression. Many thought that the main stumbling block to the law was the provision that New York–

breds must be sired by New York–based stallions, arguing that it would be difficult to win such prominent races as the Triple Crown or Breeders' Cup events unless New York breeders would be allowed access to the services of stallions in other states, particularly Kentucky.

This need was addressed when the legislature enacted L. 1994 Chapter 282, amending the Thoroughbred Breeding and Development Law to allow state breeding farms to ship broodmares out of New York to be serviced by stallions in other states, as long as the resulting foal was born in New York. In one memorandum in the law's bill jacket, the breeding situation in New York was described: "In 1987 there were over 500 active thoroughbred farms in New York—today there are fewer than 350; in 1987 there were 200 stallions standing in New York State—today there are fewer than 150; in 1987 over 2500 thoroughbreds were born in New York—this year there will be less than 1000."[2] A memorandum in the bill jacket noted that the bill was "the result of long and at times difficult discussions among the Executive, the Legislature and representatives of every segment of the racing industry."[3] Although some breeding farms in the state disliked the bill, arguing that it would financially benefit breeders in other states, it had the important approval of the law firm of Bogdan and Faist, which represented New York Thoroughbred Breeders Inc.[4]

The first indications of the salubrious effect of the new amendment were the electrifying wins of Funny Cide in the 2003 Kentucky Derby and Preakness. He was sired by Kentucky-based stallion Distorted Humor.

Author's note: In my earlier book, *From American Eclipse to Silent Screen: An Early History of New York–Breds*, I chronicled the outstanding New York–breds that raced before the incentives of the 1973 law. The present book discusses the horses whose owners benefited from that law, unfortunately not including Sackatoga's Tiz the Law and other notable New York–breds that raced after 2018.

Chapter 1

HORSES BORN 1973–1979

FIO RITO c. (1975; DREAMING NATIVE—SEAGRET, BY SEA CHARGER)

Breeder/Owner: Ray LeCesse
Trainer: Mike Ferraro
Jockey: Leslie Hulet
Career Statistics: 50 starts, 28 wins, 8 seconds, 6 thirds, $584,142

The first horse to gain national recognition under the New York State's new breeding law was Fio Rito. His owner, Ray LeCesse, was a building contractor from Rochester who had gotten involved in Thoroughbreds as a hobby, racing them at nearby Finger Lakes Race Track. He bought twenty-eight acres of land one mile from Finger Lakes and built a facility for training his horses. LeCesse described how he acquired Fio Rito: "So one day Doc Joe O'Shea asked me if it would be all right to have a horse auction there at the farm, and I said sure. Since it was my place, I went to the auction, and just to help the auctioneer, I bid on some of the horses. Well, on one of them the auctioneer dropped the hammer on me, and I wound up with this mare for $2,300."[5]

The mare, a former $1,500 claimer named Seagret, was in foal by the late stallion Dreaming Native, another former $1,500 claimer. The result was Fio Rito, named for a bandleader who was a friend of LeCesse's.

For the first four years of his career, Fio Rito made a good living racing against New York–breds at Finger Lakes, with occasional forays to New York Racing Association tracks. Most of his earnings were enriched by the state's Thoroughbred Breeding and Development Fund. Although he had a slow beginning as a 2-year-old in 1977, winning just one race in nine starts with earnings of $11,325 (which was still $9,000 more than LeCesse paid for the horse), he became a money machine during his next three years, winning $65,656, $55,200 and $192,309. All his stakes wins were restricted to New York–breds, including the 1978 Albany Handicap; the 1980 Genesee Valley; the Hudson, Bertram F. Bongard and Wadsworth Memorial Cup Handicaps; and the Joe Palmer and Alex Robb Stakes. In the Wadsworth, he was assigned a punishing 138 pounds and won by 5½ lengths.

By the summer of 1981, Fio Rito's name had become known to few race fans outside New York State. This changed dramatically on August 1 when he ran in the Whitney Stakes (gr.1) at Saratoga at odds of 10-1. The most prominent of his opponents was Rokeby Stables Winter's Tale, the 3-2 favorite that had finished second to the great John Henry

Fio Rito, the gray, Leslie Hulet up, right after winning the 1981 Whitney. Winter's Tale is on the rail. *Michele Williams.*

1980 NEW YORK HORSE OF THE YEAR
Fio Rito
1981 WHITNEY STAKES WINNER
1981 MICHIGAN MILE WINNER

Fio Rito advertisement, Leslie Hulet up, at Finger Lakes. *Courtesy of the National Museum of Racing and Hall of Fame.*

in the 1979 Eclipse Award for champion handicap horse. Other notables included Ring of Light, The Liberal Member and Noble Nashua. Those who thought that Fio Rito had little chance, including this writer, were even more derisive when he broke out of the gate prematurely. Luckily, assistant starter Jim Tsitsiragos held on to the reins, and after dragging him several yards, Fio Rito stopped and was reloaded into the starting gate. With regular rider Leslie Hulet in the irons, he led the field in his usual front-running style, but to the amazement of all, he was able to hold off the late-charging Winter's Tale to win by a neck. According to news reports, Mr. Tsitsiragos was handsomely rewarded for his efforts.

The effect of Fio Rito's win was noted by turf writer Andy Beyer:

> *Among the members of the racing and breeding aristocracy who congregate* [at Saratoga], *horses bred in New York State are somewhat of a standing joke....At least, that was the case until today, when Fio Rito, a humble New York–bred based at humble Finger Lakes Race Track, whipped all*

the elegantly pedigreed rivals in the prestigious $175,500 Whitney Stakes handicap at Saratoga.[6]

Two weeks later, Fio Rito won another open company stake, taking the Michigan Mile at Detroit as the 4-5 favorite. The fairy tale ended on September 5 when he finished eighth in the Woodward Stakes (gr.1) at Belmont Park. Fio Rito led until the half-mile pole, when he abruptly fell back. It was later disclosed that he injured an ankle during the race and was retired. His earnings for 1981 were $261,212.

Naskra's Breeze g. (1977; Naskra—Tropical Heat, by Tropical Season)

Breeder: Milfer Farm (Chester C. Davis)
Owner: Broadmoor Stable (Dr. Joe Crotty and Joe Morrissey)
Trainer: Phil Johnson
Jockey: Jean-Luc Samyn
Career Statistics: 37 starts, 15 wins, 9 seconds, 3 thirds, $705,232

After placing in his only start in 1979, Naskra's Breeze had a successful season in 1980, winning five of his twelve starts, all New York–bred races, with earnings of $112,832. Midway through the 1981 season, his career took a sharp turn upward when he won his first start on the turf in the West Point Handicap for New York–breds at Saratoga. Although many would credit Johnson for the successful switch in surfaces, he claimed that it was only because he couldn't find a long-distance race on the dirt. "That's where the genius comes in. None of the usual reasons. His feet are small, not large. He hasn't a long stride, he's just a neat little horse, and he tries hard."[7]

Naskra's Breeze had found his best surface. He followed his successful turf debut with a win in the Brighton Beach Handicap (gr.3T). Later, the State Racing and Wagering Board took away his purse money and suspended Johnson for sixty days after a tranquilizer was found in Naskra's Breeze. Johnson bitterly disputed the ruling for sixteen months.

The year 1982 was Naska's Breeze's last and most successful season. After winning his first four races of the year, including the Kingston Handicap for New York–breds, he traveled to Atlantic City to run in the $1\frac{3}{16}$-mile United

Nations Handicap (gr.1T). The race was described as "one of the best balanced fields ever for it. At 13, it also was one of the largest fields in recent years, with all but one horse having won or placed in stakes."[8] Despite the stiff competition, Naskra's Breeze won by 5 lengths at odds of 5-1. His next race was an eighth in the Arlington Million (gr.1T) on a hard surface, which was not to the gelding's liking. On September 19, he finished second in the 1¼-mile Manhattan Handicap (gr.2T), 6 lengths behind Sprink, to whom he conceded six pounds. Two weeks later, he won the Man o' War Stakes (gr.1T) as the 2-1 favorite, narrowly defeating Sprink while taking advantage of the equal weights and the extra 1-furlong distance. Finishing third was fellow New York–bred and 3-1 second favorite Thunder Puddles. After the Man o' War, Steve Crist declared that Naskra's Breeze had become "the first New York–bred horse with a legitimate chance of winning an Eclipse Award."[9]

Dreams of an Eclipse Award vanished when Naskra's Breeze ended his season by finishing second in the 1½-mile Turf Classic (gr.1T) at Aqueduct, eighth in the second division of the Hollywood Turf Cup and second as the favorite in the Walter Haight Handicap at Laurel. His 1982 earnings were $448,753.

CUPECOY'S JOY F. (1979; NORTHERLY—LADY ALBA, BY ALSINA)

Breeder: Robert Perez
Owner: Ri-Ma-Ro Stable (Robert Perez and Robert De Filippis)
Trainer: Alfredo Callejas
Jockey: Angel Santiago
Career Statistics: 22 starts, 6 wins, 7 seconds, 4 thirds, $377,960

With the exception of the Tree Top Stakes at Aqueduct, Cupecoy Joy's 2-year-old season was limited to New York–bred competition, with her one stakes win coming in the East View. She began her 3-year-old season by finishing second in the 6-furlong Rosetown Stakes at Aqueduct. After two wins and two places in sprints, she stepped up in both class and distance when she traveled to Latonia Park in Kentucky to run in the 1¹⁄₁₆-mile Jim Beam Spiral Stakes for Kentucky Derby aspirants. She finished third at odds of 9-1, which was good enough to encourage Perez to enter her in the Kentucky Derby on May 1. The only filly of the nineteen horses entered in the Derby, she was one of the eight field horses that went off at 8-1. Taking the early lead, as was her usual style, she began to drop back after a mile and finished tenth. Despite her poor showing in the Derby, Perez had planned to enter her in the Preakness, but mercifully she was scratched when Perez didn't like the seats assigned to him by the Maryland Jockey Club.

Two and a half weeks later, she finished second against New York–bred males in the Albany Handicap. Five days later, she was entered in the one-mile Acorn Stakes (g.1), the first leg in NYRA's Filly Triple Crown. Although she was facing most of the top 3-year-old fillies on the East Coast, she won by 2¾ lengths in her usual gate-to-wire fashion. Her time of 1:34 1/5 was the fastest in the stake's fifty-two-year history.

Her next race was the second leg of the Filly Triple Crown, the 1⅛-mile Mother Goose Stakes (gr.1). Although she had never run that distance, the bettors wisely took heed of her performance two weeks before and made her the 6-5 favorite. She won by ¾ of a length without being extended by Santiago. Enthused *Blood-Horse* correspondent William H. Rudy, "Cupecoy's Joy again had made a parade out of a major contest between the best fillies in training in New York."[10] As befitting her fame, she was on the cover of the June 26 *Blood-Horse*.

The last leg of the Filly Triple Crown, the 1½-mile Coaching Club American Oaks (gr.1), was on June 26. An article by Steve Crist in the *New York Times* cautioned that "Cupecoy's Joy, as brilliantly fast as she is, may have a great deal of trouble stretching her speed over a mile and a half in the Oaks. Christmas Past would probably have passed her in another eighth of a mile yesterday, and others were gaining strongly down the stretch."[11] That article was particularly prescient, as Cupecoy's Joy, the slight favorite at 5-2, lost to 2.60-1 Christmas Past by 6 lengths. The Mother Goose would be the last win of Cupecoy Joy's career, while Christmas Past, who had lost the Acorn and Mother Goose, would go on to win the Eclipse Award for 3-year-old fillies.

On July 24, Cupecoy's Joy finished last in the second division of the Sheepshead Bay Handicap (gr.2T). Despite the fact that she had never run on the turf and had never faced older horses, the bettors made her the 2-1 favorite. After the race, it was discovered that she had sustained a severe cut to her left foreleg, requiring surgery. The last race of her career, the Meadowlands Cup (gr.2) was another last, although that result should not have been a surprise. She was a 3-year-old filly in a race against older male horses, including John Henry, and her distance limitations were prominent in the 1¼-mile race. She never raced again, but for one month she was considered the best 3-year-old filly on the East Coast.

Thunder Puddles c. (1979; Speak John—Big Breeze, by Delta Judge)

Breeder/Owner: Rockwood Stable (Dr. Robert S. Boggiano and Herbert Schwartz)
Trainer: John Campo
Jockey: Angel Cordero Jr.
Career Statistics: 25 starts, 7 wins, 5 places, 5 thirds, $791,998

Thunder Puddles, like Naskra's Breeze, had some success on the main track but found his true calling when he was switched to the turf. After winning one of six starts in 1981, he won several more races on the dirt in 1982 before taking an allowance race on the turf at Belmont Park. On August 25, he won the restricted West Point Handicap on the turf at Saratoga by 10 lengths, and grass would remain his specialty. His next race was his first graded stakes win, taking the 1³/₁₆-mile Rutgers Handicap (gr.2T) at the Meadowlands at odds of 4-1. Finishing fourth was Majesty's Prince, who would later become one of the best turf horses in the country. Thunder Puddles's time of 2.13 2/5 was two-fifths of a second off the track record for the distance,

Although he lost his next three races, all Grade 1s, he was competitive in all of them. He finished third to the 4-year-old New York–bred Naskra's Breeze in the Man o' War Stakes at Belmont, second to Majesty's Prince in the Rothman's International at Woodbine and third to April Run and Majesty's Prince in the Washington, D.C. International, both on the turf, and closed out the season on the West Coast by finishing seventh in the second division of the Hollywood Turf Cup (gr.1T). Even in that race, he only lost by 5 lengths, and he finished ahead of Naskra's Breeze, who finished tenth. Thunder Puddles's earnings in 1982 were $294,078.

He continued racing against some of the best turf horses in the country in 1983. He only had two wins that year, those coming in the Kingston for New York–breds and the second division of the Red Smith Handicap (gr.2T). In the latter, he defeated the major stakes winner and the 3-2 favorite Open Call. In the Sword Dancer Stakes (gr.2T) at Belmont Park, he faced a field that had grossed $524,000 in purse money for the year. The winner was his nemesis, Majesty's Prince. Hush Dear finished second but was disqualified, with Thunder Puddles moving up to second. His other two seconds were in the 1½-mile Rothmans International (gr.1T) at Woodbine and the 1½-mile Turf Classic (gr.1T) at Aqueduct. The winner of both races was the sensational French-bred filly All Along, who had previously won the prestigious Prix de L'Arc de Triomphe (gr.1T) against males and was later inducted into the National Hall of Fame. Thunder Puddles only lost the Rothman's International by 2 lengths at odds of 22-1, with Majesty's Prince third. He finished fourth in the Bowling Green Handicap (gr.2T) at Belmont, but he was only 2 lengths behind the 3-2 favorite Tantalizing. In the Arlington Million (gr.1T), he finished fourth again, only 2 lengths behind the winner, Tolomeo, as well as John Henry and Nijinsky's Secret. Although he only won two races in 1983, he managed to earn $456,896. He was retired after the 1983 season to enter stud duty.

Chapter 2

HORSES BORN 1980–1989

WIN G. (1980; BARACHOIS—PAR CI PAR LA, BY BUCKPASSER)

Breeder: Robert G. Wehle
Owners: Sally Bailie; Paul Cornman and Fred Ephraim
Trainer: Sally Bailie
Jockeys: Anthony Graell and Richard Migliore
Career Statistics: 44 starts, 14 wins, 10 seconds, 3 thirds, $1,408,980

Win was purchased by Sally Bailie in August 1982 for $8,000 at the Fasig-Tipton sale for 2-year-olds in training at Saratoga as a favor when a friend had made the winning bid on him by mistake. In September 1983, handicapper Paul Cornman and Frederick A. Ephraim joined her as partners, with each getting one-third of the horse.

After an off-the-board effort in his only start in 1982 and a series of poor performances on the dirt, it was decided that, based on his breeding, he might be better on the grass. On September 18, he finished second in the 1½-mile Lawrence Realization (gr.2T) for 3-year-olds at Belmont Park, followed on September 29 by a win in the first division of the 1⅜-mile Rutgers Stakes (gr.2T) at the Meadowlands, with Bounding Basque second and future turf star Hero's Honor third. Win closed out his sophomore season with a fourth in the first division of the Knickerbocker Handicap (gr.3T) at Aqueduct.

In 1984, Win became one of the top turf horses on the East Coast and arguably the most accomplished New York–bred since Questionnaire and Mr. Right. His first stakes try of the year came in the 1¼-mile Red Smith Handicap (gr.2T), where he finished a distant second to Hero's Honor, who he had defeated in the previous year's Rutgers. He then took three graded stakes in a row: the Tidal Handicap (gr.2T) at Belmont Park, which was switched from the turf to the sloppy main course; the 1⅛-mile Bernard Baruch Handicap (gr.2T) at Saratoga, with Cozzene third; and the 1¼-mile Manhattan Handicap (gr.1T) as the slight favorite at 3-1.

Although he didn't win other stakes race that year, he was still competitive in all his losses. On September 8, he finished second to the multi-stakes-winning Majesty's Prince in the Man o' War Stakes (gr.1T). Notable among the also-rans was the filly Sabin, the even-money favorite that had won nine stakes that year. Two weeks later, Win finished second in the Turf Classic (gr.1T) at Belmont Park in what might have been the best race of his career. He lost by a neck at odds of 9-1 to the even-money favorite, the future Hall of Fame inductee John Henry. Both horses were just two ticks off the track record for the distance set by Secretariat. Finishing third, 4 lengths behind Win, was old foe Majesty's Prince at 4-1. Checking in fourth was another future Hall of Fame inductee, the filly All Along. Win closed out the year with a third at odds of 7-2 in the Ballentine's Scotch Classic Handicap at the Meadowlands. Although the race was ungraded because of its inaugural running, it included John Henry, the winner and 3-5 favorite; Who's for Dinner, winner of the Arlington (gr.1T) and Kelso (gr.3T) Handicaps, second at 10-1; and Hero's Honor, winner of the Fort Marcy (gr.3T), Red Smith (gr.2T), Bowling Green (gr.1T) and United Nations (gr.1T) Handicaps, seventh. Win's earnings in 1984 were $512,805.

Because of a dispute among the three owners over who would be the managing partner, only one of Win's first four starts in 1985 was a stake, that being the Tidal Handicap (gr.2T), in which he finished sixth. A trip to Saratoga showed him at his old form when he won the Bernard Baruch Handicap (gr.2T) for the second year in a row, with that year's eventual turf champion, Cozzene, a neck behind in second.

The next stop for Win was the 1¼-mile Manhattan Handicap (gr.1T) on September 1 at Belmont Park. The winner was the French campaigner Cool, who enjoyed a fourteen-pound advantage over Win, the favorite and highweight in the race. Three weeks later, Win once again finished second in a Grade 1 race, this time the 1½-mile Turf Classic at Belmont Park. The surprise winner was Nobel Fighter, the only 3-year-old in the race—his 1985 record of one win in eight starts in France was reflected in his 55-1 odds. Once again, Win was the favorite, this time at even money. Noble Fighter's time was only one-fifth of a second slower than the stakes record of 2:25 2/5, set by John Henry when he beat Win by a neck in the 1984 edition of the Turf Classic. On October 12, Win and Noble Fighter hooked up again in the Man o' War Stakes (gr.1T), with both going off as the 2-1 favorites. This time, Win prevailed, winning by a head, with Noble Fighter finishing a distant sixth. That victory made Win the first New York–bred millionaire and underlined the statement in the *Blood-Horse* that "[i]f there is a top grass runner in the United States this year, many New Yorkers think it is Sally Bailie's Win."[12] On November 3, Win won the first division of the inaugural running of the 1-mile Shergar Stakes at Aqueduct as the 3-5 favorite.

Win lost the last two races in 1985, but neither diminished his reputation. A heavy rain was the culprit in his finishing a badly beaten fifth in the Washington, D.C. International (gr.1T) over a soft course. In his last race of the year, Win finished second in the Hollywood Turf Cup (gr.1T) at odds of 7-1. The winner at 23-1 was Zoffany, a horse Win had beaten by 15 lengths in the Man o' War. Checking in third was Vanlandingham, the winner of the Washington, D.C. International (gr.1T). Win earned $655,156 in 1985, not bad for a horse that went into the Bernard Baruch on August 11 with one allowance win in four starts. His handlers had expected that Win would be able to return to racing, but a series of minor injuries and bowed tendons in both legs kept him on the shelf until the early months of 1989. On April 7, 1989, he returned to the races after an absence of thirty-eight months, finishing fifth in an allowance race on the main track. After another losing effort, he returned to the turf on May 12, winning an allowance race. On June 3, 1989, he finished fourth in the Red Smith Handicap (gr.1T) at odds of 6-1. After finishing third in an allowance race, it was announced that an inflamed suspensory in his left front leg had forced his retirement.

Slewpy c. (1980; Seattle Slew—Rare Bouquet, by Prince John)

Breeder: Seminole Syndicate (Dr. and Mrs. Jim Hill, Mr. and Mrs. Mickey Taylor)
Owner: Equusequity (Dr. and Mrs. Jim Hill, Mr. and Mrs. Mickey Taylor, et al.)
Trainer: Sidney Watters Jr.
Jockey: Angel Cordero Jr.
Career Statistics: 21 starts, 8 wins, 2 seconds, 1 third, $720,240

Although Slewpy appeared often in his native state, his favorite track was the Meadowlands in New Jersey. His main owners were the same people who owned his sire, Triple Crown winner Seattle Slew.

When Slewpy broke his maiden in his first start at Belmont Park, he became the first of Seattle Slew's progeny to win a race. He won his next start, the Empire Stakes for 2-year-olds, followed by off-the-board performances in the Hopeful (gr.1) at Saratoga, the Cowdin (gr.2) at Belmont and the Breeders' Futurity (gr.2) at Keeneland. The last particularly bothered Sidney Watters Jr., since he finished seventh, losing by 18 lengths. Despite his misgivings, he entered him in the $326,500, 1 1/16-mile Young America (gr.1) on November 4 at the Meadowlands. Slewpy turned in the best performance of his young

Slewpy, Jeffrey Fell up, after winning the 1986 Empire Stakes. *Michele Williams.*

career, taking the race by $3\frac{1}{4}$ lengths. Finishing fourth was the undefeated 2-5 favorite Copelan, who had beaten Slewpy in the Hopeful. It was also the first of four races Slewpy would win at the Meadowlands. His 1982 earnings were $244,140.

Slewpy began 1983 with a third in the Louisiana Derby (gr.2) and fifth in the Wood Memorial (gr.1). After finishing second in the New York–bred Kingston Stakes on the turf, his handlers shipped him over to England for the classic Epsom Derby (gr.1T), where he finished seventeenth on a soft turf course. When he arrived back in the United States, he returned to New Jersey to run in the Paterson Handicap (gr.2) for 3-year-olds and up at the Meadowlands after earlier winning an allowance race at that same track. The result was a first by a neck over Bounding Basque. Three weeks later, he returned to his favorite track to contest the Meadowlands Cup (gr.1) for 3-year-olds and up at $1\frac{1}{4}$ miles, where he was only a lukewarm 3-1 favorite. He won by a neck, improving his Meadowlands record to a perfect four for four. His 1983 earnings amounted to $418,868.

Slewpy had one win in four starts in 1984, the Kingston Handicap for New York–breds, retiring after sustaining a suspensory ligament in that race.

At the Threshold c. (1981; Norcliffe—Winver, by Al Hattab)

Breeder: Raymond Karlinsky; Robert and Arthur Levien
Owner: H.B. Bishop; W. Cal Partee
Trainer: W.C. Smiley; Lynn Whiting
Jockey: Eddie Maple
Career Statistics: 18 starts, 9 wins, 2 seconds, 5 thirds, $695,930

At the Threshold only ran one of his eighteen career starts in his native state. He was sold as a yearling in Kentucky and spent most of his freshman season in that state. After he was purchased by W. Cal Partee for $150,000 in November 1983, he was shipped to New York with new trainer Lynn Whiting, where he ended the season by winning the Ashley T. Cole for 2-year-old New York–breds. The wisdom in that change of venue was shown by the $70,200 he won in the Ashley T. Cole compared to the $27,435 he earned in his eight races in Kentucky, including thirds in the Kentucky Special at Latonia and the Iroquois Stakes at Churchill Downs.

When his 1983 season concluded, At the Threshold was sent to Arkansas to rest and train for his 3-year-old season. After a win and a show in two overnight handicaps at Oaklawn Park, he went to Kentucky for the $300,000 added Jim Beam Stakes (gr.3) at Latonia, winning by a length at odds of 7-2. His connections were beginning to smell roses. He was shipped to Arkansas for the 1⅛-mile Arkansas Derby (gr.1) at Oaklawn Park, where he finished fourth at odds of 7-2, with the filly Althea winning by 7 lengths. Finishing third was the 3-2 favorite Gate Dancer.

At the Threshold's next race was the Kentucky Derby (gr.1), where he finished an impressive third at odds of 37-1, with the ill-fated Swale the winner at 7-2. Finishing seventh was future older filly/mare champion Life's Magic, the 5-2 favorite with her entry mate, Althea, who finished seventeenth. Rather than racing in the Preakness, Whiting elected to enter him in the Pennsylvania Derby (gr.2), where, as the even-money favorite, he lost by a head to the 3-2 second choice Morning Bob. Although Whiting had planned to enter him in the Belmont Stakes, that race was scrapped in favor of the Ohio Derby (gr.2) at Thistledown, which he won by 3 lengths at odds of 9-10.

From Ohio, he traveled to Chicago, where on June 30 he won the Arlington Classic (gr.1) for 3-year-olds despite conceding twelve pounds to the other seven horses in the field. Although the weight assignment bothered Whiting, it did not deter the bettors, who wisely made him the 2-5 favorite. Three weeks later, he won the Arlington Derby (gr.1) in a dead heat with 24-1 High Alexander. As in the Classic, he was the 2-5 favorite, he was the highweight with 126 pounds and he even had the same jockey, Pat Day. After the race, Whiting discovered that At the Threshold had bled. Although he was scheduled to race in the Super Derby on September 22 at Louisiana Downs, Pardee decided to retire him to stud duty at Southland Farm near Ocala, Florida. His 1984 earnings were $598,295.

An article in the *Blood-Horse* with Mr. Partee revealed the unpredictable nature of the sport, especially the breeding end of it. "For $150,000, Whiting and Partee figured they had obtained a nice little sprinter that could win some minor stakes races."[13]

QUEEN ALEXANDRA F. (1982; DETERMINED KING— VICTORIA BEAUTY, BY BOLD NATIVE)

Breeder: Ocala Stud
Owner: Morton Rosenthal
Trainers: Phil Johnson; George M. Baker
Jockey: Don Brumfield
Career Statistics: 46 starts, 19 wins, 8 seconds, 5 thirds, $1,034,144

Queen Alexandra's career was enhanced when her base of operations was changed from New York to the Midwest. At ages two and three, she raced mainly in New York–bred races, her only stakes win coming in the 1984 East View at Aqueduct. In December 1985, after a winless 3-year-old season, Phil Johnson shipped her to George Baker, another trainer employed by Rosenthal, believing that she would do better in the South and Midwest. This judgment is one small indication why Johnson was inducted into the National Hall of Fame, for it transformed Queen Alexandra from a mediocre horse to one of the most respected fillies and mares in the country.

In 1986, a filly that could only win one restricted stakes race in two years of racing in the Empire State won stakes in Churchill Downs and Ellis Park in Kentucky and Fairmount and Arlington Parks in Illinois. After finishing second in the Latonia Breeders' Cup and fourth in the Locust Grove Handicap at Churchill Downs, she won five stakes in a row, beginning with the Fleur de Lis Handicap on June 1 at Churchill Downs, followed by the Ellis Park Breeders' Cup Handicap, the Breeders' Handicap at Fairmount Park and the Coca Cola Centennial at Ellis Park, all ungraded. That lack was remedied on August 30 when she took the Arlington Matron Handicap (gr.2). After finishing fourth in the Spinster (gr.1) at Keeneland, she won the Falls City Handicap (gr.3) at Churchill Downs. She ended her 1986 season with earnings of $461,926—not one cent coming from New York.

Queen Alexandra had a slow beginning in her 1987 season at Oaklawn Park, where she finished second in the Pippin and Oaklawn Breeders' Cup Handicaps and third in the Apple Blossom Handicap (gr.1). In the last two, she was beaten by North Sider, that year's champion older filly and mare. She ended her losing streak on Kentucky Derby Day when she won the $150,000 added Louisville Budweiser Breeders' Cup at Churchill Down at 11-1, with North Sider finishing fourth. She followed that with a victory in the $210,000 Sixty Sails Handicap (gr.3) at Sportsman Park in Chicago, winning by 6 lengths as the 7-5 favorite and 123-pound heavyweight.

Her season ended prematurely on June 14 when she stumbled out of the gate in the Fleur de Lis, wrenching her ankle and suffering a slight tear of a suspensory ligament. Her earnings for 1987 amounted to $344,129. She also finished tied for third, two pounds behind North Sider, in the 4-years-old and up fillies and mares division of the Experimental Free Handicap.

She had an abbreviated final 1988 season, winning the Wayward Lass at Tampa Bay Downs and an allowance race and finishing second in the Rampart (gr.2) and Oaklawn Budweiser Breeders' Cup Handicaps in eight starts. She was the second New York–bred to retire a millionaire.

WANDERKIN G. (1983; DEWAN—PLUM'S SISTER, BY QUADRANGLE)

Breeder: Flying Zee Stables (Carl Lizza Jr. and Marie Hochwrieter)
Owners: Flying Zee Stables; Poma Stable (James Meceda, Judson Posa and
*   Rose Apree)*
Trainers: Richard O'Connell; Louis Meittinis
Jockey: no main jockey
Career Statistics: 99 starts, 21 wins, 14 seconds, 21 thirds, $937,517

The gelding turf specialist Wanderkin campaigned for eight seasons. Unraced at two, he began his career under the ownership of his breeders, Flying Zee Stables, and was trained by Richard O'Connell. He earned $50,640 from eight starts in 1986, and on August 17, 1987, he was purchased by O'Connell for $55,000 at a dispersal sale on behalf of the newly formed Poma Stable, which retained O'Connell as his trainer. Wanderkin rewarded his new connections when one week after the sale he won his first stake, taking the first division of the restricted West Point Handicap on the turf at Saratoga. Later that year, on November 3, he finished third in the Knickerbocker Handicap (gr.3T) at Aqueduct. He earned $172,466 from eighteen starts in 1987.

Wanderkin began 1988 by finishing second in the Kingston Stakes for New York–breds on the turf at Aqueduct. Five days later, he finished off the board in the Fort Marcy Handicap (gr.3T), followed on June 3 by a handicap win. One week later, he won his first open stakes, taking the Blue Larkspur on the turf at Belmont Park. On July 4, he won his first graded stakes, taking the Poker (gr.3T) at Belmont. On July 20, he ran

Wanderkin in the paddock at Belmont Park prior to 1989 Kelso Handicap. *Michele Williams.*

what was arguably the best race of his career, finishing second at 5-1, 1¼ lengths behind the winner, Equalize, the second favorite at 5-2, in the United Nations Handicap at Atlantic City. Finishing third was the even-money favorite Bet Twice, famous for his Triple Crown duels with Alysheba the previous year, and finishing fifth was the 3-1 third choice, Yankee Affair. After the United Nations, Wanderkin finished fourth in the Daryl's Joy Stakes and third in the Bernard Baruch Handicap (gr.1T), both at Saratoga. He ended the year in New Jersey, finishing second in the Longfellow Handicap at Monmouth, followed by a win in the Cliff Hanger (gr.3T) at Meadowlands, beating Salem Drive by a neck while setting a new track record of 1:39 2/5 for the 1¹⁄₁₆-mile distance. The year 1988 was the most successful of his career, with five wins, three seconds and one third from fourteen starts, with earnings of $313,916.

The year 1989 was cut short by an injury, earning $108,902 from five starts. Although he only had two wins in 1990, one of them was in the Fort Lauderdale Handicap (gr.3T) at Gulfstream Park. His winter at Florida was a success, as he also finished third in the Appleton Handicap (gr.3T) and the Canadian Turf Handicap (gr.3T). He also had thirds in the Fort Marcy

Handicap (gr.3T) at Aqueduct, the Jaipur (gr.3T) at Belmont and the Daryl's Joy and West Point at Saratoga. His earnings for the year were $173,054.

In his last three years of racing, he had no graded stakes wins but managed to win $56,874 in 1991, $28,430 in 1992 and $33,238 in 1993 as a 10-year-old.

ALLEZ MI LORD C. (1983; TOM ROLFE—WHY ME LORD, BY BOLD REASONING)

Breeder/Owner: Gallagher Farm (Jerry Brody)
Trainers: Guy Harwood ; John Gosden
Jockey: no main jockey
Career Statistics: 17 starts, 7 wins, 2 seconds, 1 third, $673,273 (per Equibase)

In his first two years of racing, Allez Mi Lord (also spelled Allez Milord) ran exclusively overseas, and in his last year, he continued racing in Europe until he closed out his career in the United States.

Impressed with European training methods, Jerry Brody sent his colt to England when he was a yearling. After winning his only race as a 2-year-old, at three he became a Group 1 winner when he took the Puma Europa Preis in Germany and was named that country's champion 3-year-old colt. He ended his sophomore season by losing the rich Japan Cup to England-based Jupiter. The finish was so close that it took the Japanese officials fifteen minutes to decide who had won. According to Equibase, his 1986 his 1986 earnings came to $380,636.

In 1987, he won the Gordon Richards (gr.3) and finished second in the Brigadier (gr.2) Stakes in England before he was shipped to the United States to finish his career. His first start in the United States was in the state of his birth, the 1½-mile Turf Classic (gr.1T) at Belmont Park on a soft surface. The even-money favorite in the field was the turf champion Theatrical, with Allez Milord going off at 5-1. The American expatriate took a commanding lead despite jockey Greville Starkey's efforts to restrain him. By the final turn, he was collared by Theatrical, who continued on to a 3½-lengths win, while Allez Milord labored in last. It was later discovered that he bled in the race, and he was shipped to California, with John Gosden assuming the training duties. He was treated with Lasix, which at that time was not allowed in New York.

His first race on the West Coast was a successful one when he took the Oak Tree Invitational (gr. 1T) at Santa Anita by 2½ lengths at odds of 7-1 with Chris McCarron in the irons. The last race of his career was the Breeders' Cup Turf Classic (gr. 1T) at Hollywood Park. There was no grand finale, as Allez Milord finished eighth at odds of 7-1, with the 4-5 favorite Theatrical winning by half a length.

His 1987 earnings were $286,398. As befitting his globetrotter status, he was shipped to Japan to begin stud duty at Shadai Stud.

CHEAPSKATE G. (1983; OVERSKATE—KIMBERLY JONES, BY GOOD OLD MORT)

Breeder: Jean DiCastella DeDelley, Susie Bankard, and Mrs. Primrose Haynes
Owner: Dot Dash Stables (Jim and Joyce Vandervoot)
Trainer: Darrell Vienna
Jockey: Marco Castaneda
Career Statistics: 17 starts, 4 wins, 6 seconds, 2 thirds, $475,214

Unraced at two, Cheapskate lost his first five starts as a 3-year-old before breaking his maiden on May 31 in the 7½-furlong Emeryville Handicap on the turf at Golden Gate Field. After a second in the Sutter Handicap on the turf, he was shipped to Canterbury Downs in Minnesota to run in the inaugural $300,000 St. Paul Derby on June 2 on the dirt. The race was considered a stopover on his way to participate in the lucrative New York–bred stakes program. The favorite was the multiple Grade 1 winner Broad Brush, who, along with Rampage, winner of the Arkansas Derby(gr.2), and Bachelor Beau, winner of the Blue Grass (gr.1), were lured to the race by $100,000 in extra incentives if they finished first, second or third. Cheapskate shocked the bettors when he overtook Broad Brush at the top of the stretch to win by a nose at odds of 70-1.

After the "stopover" in Minnesota, Cheapskate continued on to New York State, where he finished second in the New York Derby at Finger Lakes and won the Albany Stakes at Saratoga, both on the dirt. He then ventured into graded stakes, finishing third at 5-1 in the Arlington Classic (gr.1) for 3-year-olds. Finishing eighth was Lac Ouimet, the favorite at 5-2. One month later, he finished in a dead heat for second in the Super Derby (gr.1) at Louisiana Downs. The winner by half a length, the 7-10 favorite Wise Times, had earlier won the Haskell (gr.1) and Travers (gr.1) Stakes. Cheapskate closed out the season by winning his only graded stakes, the Affirmed Handicap (gr.3) at Hollywood Park. He finished off the board in his only start in 1987 and never raced again.

GRECIAN FLIGHT F. (1984; CORMORANT—GREEN GREEK, BY TICKET)

Breeder/Owner: Henry C.B. Lindh
Trainer: Joe Pierce Jr.
Jockeys: Craig Perret and Chris Antley
Career Statistics: 40 starts, 21 wins, 6 seconds, 3 thirds, $1,320,215

Grecian Flight had an abbreviated 2-year-old season cut short by a cracked shin bone. She started four times, with her only win in open company coming in the Holly Stakes at the Meadowlands. Her one loss came in the Tempted Stakes (gr.3) when she finished second by a neck to Silent Turn.

She became a middle-distance star in 1987, starting nine times, all stakes, and winning four. After beginning the year by winning the New York–bred Montauk and Bouwerie Stakes, she suffered the first two off-the-board defeats of her career when she finished eighth by 17 lengths in the Ashland (gr.1) at Keeneland and fourth in the Comely Stakes (gr.3) at Aqueduct. After the Comely, Joe Pierce decided to change her front-running style to coming off the pace. In another change, he replaced jockeys from Chris Antley and Randy Romero to Craig Perret.

The results of the changes were dramatic when she won her next race, the Black-Eyed Susan Stakes (gr.2) at Pimlico, by 3 lengths after coming back from fourth. On May 3, she won the one-mile Acorn Stakes (gr.1) at Belmont Park at odds of 11-1. Once again, she rallied from fourth, winning by 1½ lengths from a hard-charging Fiesta Gal. The latter's entrymate, Chic Shirine, who had beaten Grecian Flight so decisively in the Ashland, finished fourth. Among the also-rans were the even-money favorite Devil's Bride, tenth, and Tappiano, 4-1, eleventh.

The Acorn would be her last win of the year, as she finished second in the 1⅛-mile Mother Goose Stakes (gr.1), fourth in the 1½-mile Coaching Club American Oaks (gr.1) and third in the 1⅛-mile Monmouth Oaks (gr.1), her last race of the year. She won a total of $394,766 for the year and was

Grecian Flight, Craig Perret up, in the post parade for the 1987 Mother Goose. *Michele Williams.*

assigned 119 pounds in the Free Experimental Handicap, with only Personal Ensign (124), Sacchuista (124) and Fiesta Gal (120) rated higher.

Grecian Flight's 1988 season included two graded stakes wins, the Vagrancy Handicap (gr.3) at 7 furlongs, going off as the 2-1 favorite against such stars as Tappiano and Cadillacing, and the Woodbine Breeders' Cup Handicap (gr.2). Her other stakes win came in the Hyde Park Handicap for New York–breds, and she also finished a well-beaten second to future National Hall of Fame inductee Personal Ensign in the Molly Pitcher Handicap (gr.2) at Monmouth Park. She ended the season with earnings of $337,145.

She began the 1989 season with two allowance wins and a third in the Shuvee Handicap (gr.1) at Belmont Park. On June 11, she won the one-mile, seventy-yards Monmouth Park Breeders' Cup Handicap (gr.3) by 4 lengths, equaling the track record of 1:39 1/5. After a third in the Molly Pitcher Handicap (gr.2) and a fifth in the Budweiser Stakes at Fairmount Park, she won the Burlington County Stakes at the Meadowlands and finished second to Kentucky Derby winner Winning Colors in the Turfway-Budweiser Breeders' Cup. On October 29, she won the 7-furlong First Flight Handicap (gr.3) by a neck at Aqueduct, putting her over the million-dollar mark in earnings. She ended her season with wins in the Straight Deal Handicap at Laurel Park and the New York–bred Iroquois Stakes and Ticonderoga Handicap, giving her earnings of $459,126. After one place in two starts in 1990, she was retired.

BURYYOURBELIEF F. (1984; BELIEVE IT—BURY THE HATCHET, BY TOM ROLFE)

Breeders: Bray Terminals and Dana Bray Jr.
Owner: Dana Bray Jr.
Trainer: Laz Barrera
Jockey: Alex Solis
Career Statistics: 21 starts, 3 wins, 5 seconds, 3 thirds, $308,879

Buryyourbelief began her career in California, three thousand miles from Dana Bray Jr.'s home in Glens Falls, New York. After breaking her maiden in her third start in 1986, she won one of three allowance races before finishing second in the Santa Ysabel Stakes and Santa Anita Oaks (gr.1) and the Ashland Stakes (gr.1) at Keeneland. In her next start, she broke her seconditis in a big way when she won the Kentucky Oaks (gr.1) by 2¾ lengths at odds of 8-1. Finishing behind her were star fillies Hometown Queen (5-2, second), Very Subtle (9-2, sixth, a future Hall of Fame nominee as a sprinter) and Up the Apalachee (1-1, seventh). The Oaks would be the last win of her career, and on September 3, 1988, she suffered a fatal breakdown in a turf allowance at Del Mar.

FOURSTARDAVE G. (1985; COMPLIANCE—BROADWAY JOAN, BY BOLD ARIA)

Breeder: Richard Bomze
Owners: Richard Bomze and Bernard Connaughton
Trainer: Leo O'Brien
Jockeys: Richard Migliore, Mike Smith and Jose Santos
Career Statistics: 100 starts, 21 wins, 18 seconds, 16 thirds, $1,636,737

Fourstardave, the "Sultan of Saratoga," was one of the most popular horses ever to race at that historic track. His first added money win came in the Empire Stakes for 2-year-olds on the main track at Saratoga. It was the first in Fourstardave's historic string of eight consecutive years of at least one win at Saratoga. He also finished second in the New York Stallion Stakes at Belmont and Aqueduct, on both occasions losing to Ballindaggin. He ended his 2-year-old season with earnings of $216,746.

At three, he won his first open stakes when he took the $300,000 St. Paul Derby (gr.2) on the dirt at Canterbury Downs at odds of 21-1. Finishing second was 56-1 Hedevar the Gold, while the 1-2 favorite, Tejano, who had won more than $1 million as a 2-year-old, finished ninth. The first edition of the St. Paul Derby in 1986 was won by another New York–bred, Cheapskate, at odds of 72-1. Fourstardave's only other win that year came in the restricted Albany Stakes on Saratoga's dirt course. He found his favorite surface when he finished second in the Gallant Man (gr.3T) on Saratoga's turf course (although he was placed fourth by disqualification) and his third in the listed $200,000 Laurel Dash on the turf. From then on, he raced almost exclusively on the grass. In his first Grade 1 race, the Hollywood Derby (gr.1T), he finished tenth but was only 4 lengths from the winner, Silver Circus. Fourstardave won $377,139 in 1988, with $180,000 of that coming from his win in the St. Paul Derby. It would be the most lucrative year of his career, ironically the majority of that money earned on the dirt.

In 1989, he won the Poker Stakes (gr.3T) at Belmont Park and the restricted West Point Handicap at Saratoga, and he placed in the Jaipur (gr.3T), the second division of the Daryl's Joy (gr.3T) and the Fort Marcy (gr.3T). These five races show his versatility, as they ranged in distance from $1\frac{1}{16}$-miles (the Fort Marcy and Daryl's Joy) to 7 furlongs (the Jaipur). His most impressive race was the Fort Marcy, which he lost by ¾ of a length to Arlene's Valentine, with the previous year's male turf champion Sunshine Forever finishing in third, ¾ of a length behind Fourstardave. The gelding's 1989 earnings were $237,425.

Two of his four wins in 1990 came in the Jaipur Stakes at Belmont Park and the Daryl's Joy (gr.3T). The latter marked the fourth straight year he won a stakes win at Saratoga. Surprisingly, at least in retrospect, he went off at 11-1. His earnings for the year were $222,312. Although he only won two races in eleven starts in 1991, they came in the Daryl's Joy (gr.3T) and West Point Handicaps at Saratoga, making that the fifth year he won at least one stakes race at his favorite track. The year 1992 was the first since his 2-year-old season that he did not win a graded stakes, and his earnings were, for him, a paltry $125,188. His only stakes win was in the Manila in the Meadowlands, and his streak of five years with at least one stakes win at Saratoga was broken. However, an allowance win gave him six straight years of winning at least one race at that track. To the legions of Fourstardave fans who thought his career was over, 1993 proved to be a revelation. His stakes wins included the Poker (gr.3T), in which he broke the stakes record that he had set in 1989, and the Neshaminy Handicap at Philadelphia. In

Above: Fourstardave in the paddock at Belmont Park prior to the 1989 Kelso Handicap. *Michele Williams*.

Opposite: Fourstardave, race and jockey unknown. *NYRA*/Bob *Coglianese*.

the Daryl's Joy Handicap (gr.3T) at Saratoga, he finished second, 3 lengths behind the winner, future National Hall of Fame inductee Lure. He stretched his record of at least one win in a season at Saratoga to seven when he won the Calcutta Cup Handicap, in which, in addition to the purse, the owners chipped in $1,000 apiece into a winner-take-all side pool. When he crossed the finish line in front, track announcer Tom Durkin called him a "living Saratoga legend." He later won the West Point but was disqualified to fifth, a decision that enraged his many fans as well as his owner, trainer and jockey Richard Migliore.

In 1994, he was restricted to seven races, winning one. However, that one race, an allowance at Saratoga, gave him eight straight seasons at the Spa. Although it was only an allowance win, the crowd was ecstatic. "Jockey Richard Migliore gave him a slow, hero's walk back to the winner's circle.… The fans were clapping without pause and were still lining the grandstand rail minutes later to cheer him as he walked off the track. It suddenly felt a lot like Saratoga."[14] To show that he still had at least a spark of his old ability, on August 12 he finished third in the Bernard Baruch Handicap (gr.2T). Finishing ahead of him were future National Hall of Fame inductee Lure and that year's male turf champion Paradise Creek. After the race, it was discovered that he had fractured his ankle during the race. After he was retired for the season, Steve Crist described Fourstardave's impact on Saratoga: "He has never won the Kentucky Derby, a Breeders' Cup race, an Eclipse Award, or even a Grade 1 race. But for five weeks, at one track, Saratoga is a one-horse town, and that horse is Fourstardave."[15]

He raced six times in 1995, finishing out of the money in all of them, with three of those losses at his beloved Saratoga. Time and his ankle injury had taken their toll, and he was retired. His Saratoga record was nine wins, three seconds and one third from eighteen starts. In 1996, the New York Racing Association changed the name of the Daryl's Joy to the Fourstardave Handicap. In 2002, he died of a heart attack at the relatively early age of seventeen, and his body was buried in Clare Court on the Saratoga's Nelson Avenue backside.

JOE'S TAMMIE F. (1985; ZONING—FUNNY TAMMIE, BY TENTAM)

Breeders: Dominick Imperio and Laura Connelly
Owners: Suzanne Moscarelli; David Milch; J.L. Paliafito
Trainers: H. Allen Jerkens; Darrell Vienna; Jack Van Berg
Jockey: no main jockey
Career Statistics: 25 starts, 10 wins, 3 seconds, 4 thirds, $644,564

After breaking her maiden in her second start, on July 15, 1987, Joe's Tammie won her first stakes, taking the Astoria (gr.3) at Belmont Park. She was then sold to television producer David Milch. California-based Darrell Vienna was nominally her trainer, but her day-to-day activities were overseen by Greg Offender and his wife, Kim Anderson. Her next stakes appearance was in the Schuylerville (gr.2) at Saratoga, finishing second by a neck to Over All. On August 30, she won the biggest race of her career, the $331,400 Arlington-Lassie Stake (gr.1) at Arlington Park, by 2 lengths as the even-money favorite. The $186,000 she won in that race was at that time the second-highest purse ever won by a New York–bred, topped only by the $253,677 won by Allez Milord when he finished second in the 1986 Japan Cup.[16] Joe's Tammie won one other stakes races that year, the restricted East View on November 2, giving her earnings of $326,052.

Although she won $283,220 in 1989, her only stakes wins were in New York–bred races. After winning one of two races in 1990, she was retired.

Ballindaggin c. (1985; Noble Nashua—Can't Be Bothered, by Stop the Music)

Breeder: Eaton and Thorne
Owner: George Layman Jr.
Trainer: John Hertler
Jockey: no main jockey
Career Statistics: 14 starts, 4 wins, 2 seconds, 3 thirds, $946,894

Ballindaggin was hardly the most accomplished Thoroughbred in training, but he had a knack for rising to the occasion when big money was involved. His three wins in 1987 were all in New York's lucrative stallion series. He was winless in his first seven starts of 1988, with a second and a third in two New York–bred races and a third in the Longacres Derby (gr.3) near Seattle, Washington, the home state of his owner. On September 11, he took his seven-race losing streak to Woodbine in Canada for the inaugural running of the $1 million Molson Export Challenge, which was created by the Ontario Jockey Club to lure the best 3-year-olds in North America. However, as described by Neil Campbell, "There was no Winning Colors, no Forty Niner, and no Brian's Time, Seeking the Gold, or Lively One. Evening Kris was the only Grade 1 winner in the field, with Cefis, Dynaformer and Regal Classic being the only other graded stakes winner."[17] With Jose Santos in the irons, Ballindaggin battled for the lead with Regal Classic throughout the race, winning by half a length at odds of 9-1. The $600,000 (in Canadian money) was by far the largest purse won by a New York–bred at that time. On October 1, he ended his career with a third in the Pennsylvania Derby (gr.1), leaving him only $54 short of being a millionaire despite having only one graded stakes win to his name.

Fit for a Queen f. (1986; Fit to Fight—Titled, by Impressive)

Breeder: Morton Rosenthal
Owners: Guiting Stud; Henry Alexander; Heritage Farm (Warner L. Jones)
Trainers: Shug McGaughey; Steve Penrod (English trainer unknown)
Jockeys: R.D. Lopez, Jerry Bailey and Pat Day
Career Statistics: 51 starts, 13 wins, 14 seconds, 9 thirds, $1,226,429

After Fit for a Queen was sold in the summer of 1987 for $44,000 to Guiting Stud, she was shipped to England. After eighteen months of less than spectacular racing, she was bought by Henry Alexander and returned to the United States. In the winter of 1990, she began to show some potential when she was shipped to Gulfstream Park with trainer Shug McGaughey, where she finished third in the 6-furlong First Lady Handicap, second in the 7-furlong Shirley Jones Handicap (gr.3) and second in the 1^1/$_{16}$-mile Johnnie Walker Black Classic Handicap (gr.2). From Florida, she was shipped to Arkansas, where she finished third as the favorite in the 1^1/$_{16}$-mile Oaklawn Breeders' Cup Handicap (gr.3).

After that race she was sold to Churchill Downs board chairman Warner L. Jones's Hermitage Farm, with Steve Penrod taking over the training duties. After several allowance races at Churchill Downs, which would serve as her home base, she traveled to Chicago, where she won her first added-money event, the 7-furlong Chicago Breeders' Cup Handicap at Arlington Park at odds of 7-1. She also finished second in the 7-furlong Breeders' Cup Handicap and the one-mile HBPA Handicap, both at Ellis Park. She finished the year with earnings of $234,506.

In the next two years, Fit for a Queen raced against some of the best fillies and mares in the country. She also had a slight trainer change, with Steve Penrod still handling her races in Kentucky and Shug McGaughey taking over when she ran in other jurisdictions. She began 1991 in Gulfstream Park, winning an allowance race and the Sabin Breeders' Cup. After two off-the-board finishes in the Rampart and Moon Glitter Handicaps, she was shipped back to Churchill Downs, where she won her first graded stakes, the 1^1/$_{16}$-mile Louisville Breeders' Cup Handicap (gr.2), by 5 lengths. After finishing second as the 3-5 favorite in the Fleur de Lis Handicap (gr.3), she won an allowance race and the Turfway Handicap (gr.3). After a fifth-place finish to Wilderness Song in the Spinster Stakes (gr.1) at Keeneland, she traveled back to Churchill Downs to compete in the most important race of her career, the

Breeders' Cup Distaff. She finished fourth at odds of 20-1, a little less than 5 lengths from the winner, future National Hall of Fame and Canadian Hall of Fame inductee Dance Smartly, who, with her entrymate Wilderness Song, was the 1-2 favorite. Finishing second was 3-year-old Versailles Treaty, the second favorite after winning the Test (gr.1), Alabama (gr.1) and Gazelle (gr.1). Trailing Fit for a Queen in fifth was the third favorite, 5-year-old Queena, winner of the Vagrancy (gr.3), Ballerina (gr.1) and Maskette (gr.1). Wilderness Song, who had beaten Fit for a Queen in the Spinster, checked in seventh.

The Breeders' Cup Distaff was not the end of Fit for a Queen's season. One week later, on November 9, she won the Churchill Downs Breeders' Cup Handicap with old foe Wilderness Song second, 4 lengths behind. She ended the year by finishing second in the Falls City Handicap (gr.3), giving her earnings of $515,213. In the Free Experimental Handicap for 4-years-old and up fillies and mares, she was assigned 123 pounds, 2 less than the four co-highweights, including future National Hall of Fame inductee Bayakoa and Queena, who had trailed Fit for a Queen in the Breeders' Cup Distaff. Behind her with 119 pounds was future National Hall of Fame inductee Paseana.

In 1992, she won two of eight starts. Her first win was in the Rampart Handicap (gr.2) at Gulfstream Park by $5^1/_5$ lengths. Her second came in the Turfway Breeders' Cup (gr.3) on September 20, the last race of her career. It was later disclosed that at the time of the race, she was in foal to Gulch. Of her other races that year, the most notable was her second in the Apple Blossom (gr.1) at Oaklawn, $4^1/_2$ lengths behind Paseana, the 1-2 favorite. Not one of her career fifty-one starts was in New York State.

CAPADES f. (1986; OVERSKATE—MEDAL OF VALOR, BY DAMASCUS)

Breeder: Gerald A. Nielsen
Owners: Hogan Point Stable; Poma Stable
Trainer: Richard O'Connell
Jockey: Angel Cordero Jr.
Career Statistics: 27 starts, 11 wins, 9 seconds, 2 thirds, $1,051,006

Capades was a turf specialist who often beat her male counterparts as well as older fillies and mares. After one win in her first five starts in her 2-year-old season, she traveled to Maryland to train for the Selima Stakes (gr.1T) for 2-year-old fillies at Laurel Park. Just before she was to race in the Queen Empress Stakes at Laurel, her trainer, Richard O'Connell, negotiated her sale to the Poma Stable, which also employed O'Connell as a trainer. She finished second in the Queen Empress, but it gave her experience over the Laurel turf course, and on October 22, she won the Selima Stakes by 1¾ lengths at odds of 6-1. She ended her 1988 season with earnings of $207,690.

The Selima was a hint of what was to come in 1989. She began a four-race stakes winning streak on June 5 by taking the 1¹/₁₆-mile Broad Brush Stakes against males by 5½ lengths on Pimlico's turf course. Three weeks later, she won the Canterbury Oaks (gr.3T) by a neck over the favored Coolawin while carrying 124 pounds. On July 23, she won her third straight stakes by taking the first division of the New York–bred Mount Vernon at Belmont Park, and August 9, she added the 1¹/₁₆-mile Nijana Stakes (gr.2T) for 3-year-old fillies as the 4-5 favorite. On September 9, she ran in the inaugural edition of the $500,000, 1³/₁₆-mile Beverly D. Stakes at Arlington Park. She finished second, 1¾ lengths behind the even-money favorite, the 4-year-old Claire Marine, who had previously won five stakes in California. Two weeks later, she finished second again, this time in the 1¼-mile Flower Bowl Handicap (gr.1T) for 3-year-old and up fillies and mares at Belmont Park. As an indication of her status, although she was only one of two 3-year-old fillies in the race, she nevertheless went off as the 3-1 favorite. An important factor in Capades's defeat was the yielding turf course. On October 9, she returned to the winner's circle when she won the 1³/₈-mile Athenia Handicap (gr.3T) at Belmont Park. On October 22, she finished second in the 1¹/₈-mile, $300,000 All Along Stakes at Laurel Park, with the French filly Lady Winner in front by 7 lengths on a soft turf course. Her last race of the year resulted in a third in the Princess Rooney Handicap at Gulfstream Park. Although her losses in the fall probably cost her an Eclipse Award, she nevertheless had a successful and lucrative season, with earnings of $509,676. Her handlers could take solace in the 1990 Free Experimental Handicap for 3-year-olds and up fillies and mares turf, which made her the highweight with 123 pounds. She was given 3 pounds more than California-based Brown Bess, who won that year's Eclipse Award for turf fillies and mares.

Capades's 1990 season began in April. After winning two of three allowance races, she began her stakes campaign on June 16 with a win in the New York Handicap (gr.2T) by a nose over Grade 1 winner and 8-5 favorite Laugh and Be Merry, setting a new track record of 1:58 2/5 over a rock-hard turf course. On July 11, she won the Matchmaker Stakes (gr.2T) by 4¼ lengths at Atlantic City as the even-money favorite and 120 pounds highweight. Finishing second was old foe Gaily Gaily.

Next on Capades's agenda was the $500,000 Caesar's International Handicap (gr.2T), formerly called the United Nations Handicap, at Atlantic City, with Capades the only filly in the race. The purse attracted a stellar field, headed by the previous year's male grass champion, Steinlen, the favorite at 3-2; Steinlen won by 3¾ lengths, setting a new track record of 1:52. Capades did manage to finish second at 6-1, beating such stalwarts as Alwuhush (5-2, third) and Yankee Affair (5-1, sixth). Eleven days later, she finished fifth as the 2-1 favorite in the $500,000 Beverly D. Stakes at Arlington Park, starting from the 12-post position. On September 14, she finished second in the Turf Classic Stakes at the Meadowlands, and two weeks later she was retired after breaking down during a workout at Belmont Park. Turf historian Mike Veitch summed up Capades's career: "She never needed to take her track with her. She never failed to give her best against her own sex or males. And she showed on more than one occasion that she could run with the country's best turf females and bring back the biggest share of the purse."[18]

FOURSTARS ALLSTAR, C (1988; COMPLIANCE—BROADWAY JOAN, BY BOLD ARIAN)

Breeder: Richard Bomze
Owners: Richard Bomze and Phil Dileo
Trainer: Leo O'Brien
Jockey: Mike Smith
Career Statistics: 59 starts, 14 wins, 14 seconds, 8 thirds, $1,596,760

Fourstars Allstar was a full brother to Fourstardave, and like his brother, he became a turf specialist. He ran his first nine races of his 2-year-old career in maiden, allowance and minor stakes races until October 20, when he finished second in the Laurel Futurity (gr.3T). He followed that with wins in the Pilgrim Stakes (gr.3T) and restricted Damon Runyon at Aqueduct. He finished the year with earnings of $215,340.

With one outstanding exception, his record for 1991 was lackluster. However, that one race would be the most important, and the most historic, of his career. On May 18, he ran in the $393,140 Irish 2000 Guineas, winning

Fourstars Allstar, Mike Smith up, on his way to winning the 2000 Irish Guineas, Star of Gdansk second. *Healy Racing Ltd. / Allan Carter.*

by a head over Star of Gdansk at odds of 9-1, with Mike Smith aboard, to become the first horse trained in the United States to win a European classic. He won only one other race that year, an allowance on the turf, finishing the season earning $327,880, most of that coming from Ireland.

He began his 4-year-old season on April 10 with a win in the Elkhorn Stakes (gr.3T) at Keeneland. His only other win that year was in the Bernard Baruch Handicap (gr.2T) at Saratoga as the 13-10 favorite against moderate opposition. He also finished third in the Early Times Turf Classic (gr.3T) at Churchill Downs and second in the Dixie Handicap (gr.2T) at Pimlico, a half length behind multi-stakes winner Sky Classic. He earned $254,966 in 1992.

Although he only had two wins in seven starts in 1993, his earnings of $347,880 were the highest of his six-year career. His two wins came in the New Hampshire Sweepstakes Handicap (gr.3T) at Rockingham Park (he finished in a dead heat for first with Idle Son, but the latter was disqualified for interference) and the Saratoga Breeders' Cup Handicap. Perhaps the best race he ran in the United States was in the 1993 Breeders' Cup Mile (gr.1T) at Santa Anita. He finished third at 74-1, 4 lengths behind the future

National Hall of Fame inductee Lure, the even-money favorite, and 1¾ lengths behind the French star Ski Paradise. Following Fourstars Allstar were Toussaud, 11-1, winner of the Gamely (gr.1T), Wilshire (gr.2T) and America (gr.2T) Handicaps; the Irish-bred Barathea, 9-1, who would win the 1994 edition of this race; Bigstone, another Irish-bred, 12-1, winner of that year's Prix Omnium (gr.1T), Sussex (gr.1T) and Queen Elizabeth II (gr.1T) Stakes; Paradise Creek, 8-1, the 1994 champion turf male; and Flawlessly, 3-1, another future National Hall of Fame inductee. Fourstars Allstar's third-place finish was worth $120,000, his biggest payday since his win in Ireland.

He only had one win in eleven starts in 1994, but he continued to be competitive with the best turf horses in the country. He finished second to Paradise Creek in the Appleton (gr.3T) at Gulfstream Park and lost by a nose to his old nemesis Lure in the Caesar's International Handicap (gr.1T) at Atlantic City, with Star of Cozzene, a multi-graded stakes winner in 1993, in third. Despite only one win, he still managed to earn $217,028.

He might have lost a step or two in 1995, his last year of racing, but he still managed to win the Fort Marcy Handicap (gr.3T) after two previous losses, as well as his second Bernard Baruch Handicap (gr.2T) despite a soft turf course, which Leo O'Brien claimed he didn't like. He ended his career finishing seventh in the Breeders' Cup Mile (gr.1T).

After his retirement, he was sent to Ireland to take on stud duty, later moving to England. He died prematurely at the age of seventeen from a paddock accident. Although he lacked his older brother's charisma, he made $40,000 more than Fourstardave, despite appearing in forty fewer races. Turf historian Mike Veitch described him as "one of the best New York–breds of modern times."[19]

SHARED INTEREST f. (1988; PLEASANT COLONY—SURGERY, BY DR. FAGER)

Breeder/Owner: Robert S. Evans
Trainer: Scotty Schulhofer
Jockeys: Julie Krone, Jerry Bailey and Robbie Davis
Career Statistics: 23 starts, 10 wins, 5 seconds, 3 thirds, $667,610

Unraced at two, Shared Interest won her first four starts in 1991 before she was entered in the Coaching Club American Oaks (gr.1), finishing

Shared Interest, Robbie Davis up, in the paddock at Belmont Park prior to the 1993 Beldame. *Michele Williams.*

fourth, 17 lengths behind the winner, Lite Light. Her next race was the Monmouth Oaks (gr.2), in which she finished second, 1¼ lengths behind Fowda, who had previously won the Hollywood Oaks (gr.1). She ended her season with a win in the Burlington County at the Meadowlands, giving her earnings of $183,000.

She began her 4-year-old season by winning an allowance race, followed by losses in three straight Grade 1 races: sixth in the Ballerina Stakes at Saratoga; third, 7½ lengths behind Quick Mischief, in the John A. Morris Handicap at Saratoga; and fourth, 5¾ lengths behind Versailles Treaty, in the Ruffian Handicap at Belmont Park. After capturing the First Flight Handicap (gr.2) at Belmont, she finished her season by finishing eleventh behind Paseana, Versailles Treaty et al. in the Breeders' Cup Distaff (gr.1).

In 1993, her last year of racing, she only had three wins, including an allowance and handicap, but unlike her first two years, she was competitive against the best fillies and mares in the East. She began her season at Gulfstream Park by winning an allowance, followed by a fifth in the Rampart Handicap (gr.2). After traveling north to her native state, she finished second in a handicap and second in the Shuvee Handicap (gr.1), ¾ of a length behind the 7-10 favorite Turnback the Alarm, winner of the 1992 Coaching

Club American Oaks (gr.1) and Mother Goose (gr.1) and the 1993 Go for Wand (gr.1). After an easy allowance win, she traveled to Arlington Park in Chicago, finishing second in the 7-furlong Chicago Budweiser Breeders' Cup (gr.3) to Meafara, who ran second in the 1992 and 1993 Breeders' Cup Sprint. After finishing second, 2½ lengths behind You'd Be Surprised, in the Top Flight Handicap (gr.1) at Belmont Park, she ran the best race of her career, taking the Ruffian Handicap (gr.1). She was the longest shot in the five-horse field, and the horses she beat were the 3-year-old Dispute, winner of that year's Bonnie Miss (gr.2), Kentucky Oaks (gr.1) and Gazelle Handicap (gr.1); Turnback the Alarm; You'd Be Surprised; and the even-money favorite, the future National Hall of Fame inductee Paseana. She ended her career by finishing second in the Beldame Stakes (gr.1), 1½ lengths behind Dispute, and third in the First Flight Handicap (gr.2) as the even-money favorite. Her 1993 earnings were $338,210.

THUNDER RUMBLE C. (1989; THUNDER PUDDLES—LYPHETTE, BY LYPHARD)

Breeder/Owner: Dr. Konrad Widmer
Trainer: Richard O'Connell, Chris Speckart
Jockey: Herb McCauley
Career Statistics: 19 starts, 8 wins, 1 third, $1,047,552

Thunder Rumble and his sire formed a potent New York–bred father-and-son duo that rivaled Sanford Stud's Rockton (born 1897) and Mohawk II (born 1903) and James Butler's Sting (born 1921) and Questionnaire (born 1927). Thunder Rumble's 2-year-old season began on the turf, which his breeding indicated would be his best surface. However, breeding can be a fickle yardstick, to which Cigar's trainer Bill Mott could agree. He made his turf debut on October 24 at Aqueduct in a New York–bred maiden turf race as the 7-5 favorite. Contrary to the expectations of his handlers and the bettors, he bolted on the first turn and lost by 20 lengths. Two months later, he broke his maiden when he won New York–bred maiden race on Aqueduct's inner dirt track by 12¾ lengths. Thunder Rumble's true surface, dirt, had been found.

On January 12, 1992, Thunder Rumble won the 1¹/₁₆-mile Montauk Stakes for New York–breds by 4 lengths as the 2-1 favorite. Two weeks later, he won the open Count Fleet Stakes by 2 lengths, and O'Connell now had the Wood Memorial (gr.1), New York's premier race for Kentucky Derby hopefuls, in his plans. On February 15, his road to the Wood took a detour when he faded to third in the Whirlaway Breeders' Cup Stakes at Aqueduct. One month later, the Wood still remained a goal when he won the 9-furlong Gate Dancer Stakes at Aqueduct by 4 lengths. However, fate intervened when Thunder Rumble came down with a virulent fever on the day of the Wood, knocking him out of that race and the Triple Crown races.

O'Connell regrouped and set his sights on the Travers (gr.1) at Saratoga. Four months after Thunder Rumble's win in the Gate Dancer, he was entered in an allowance race on the turf at Belmont Park. His seventh-place finish finally convinced O'Connell that the turf was not in his charge's future, although he might have been thinking of the turf-to-dirt angle. Thunder Rumble was shipped to Saratoga, and on August 2, he ran in the 1⅛-mile Jim Dandy Stakes (gr.2), the traditional prep for the Travers. To the surprise of the bettors, who sent him off at odds of 24-1, he won the Jim Dandy by half a length over the second-place finisher, Dixie Brass, winner of the 1992 Metropolitan Handicap (gr.1) and Withers Stakes (gr.2). Three weeks later, Thunder Rumble won the Travers Stakes at odds of 7-1, 4½ lengths ahead of Devil His Due. Steve Crist wrote, "There was no question that the winner was by far the best, and while his handlers had been confident, they were surprised by the scope and ease of their colt's victory."[20] The rest of his 1992 season was not pretty. Two months after his Travers triumph, he finished fifth in the Woodward (gr.1), followed by a seventh and last in the Jockey Club Gold Cup (gr.1). Despite his disappointing finish, his 1992 earnings amounted to $850,902.

He injured his ankle during the running of the Jockey Club Gold Cup, which led to what Steve Crist called "23 months of defeat and despair."[21] He missed the entire 1993 season, and when O'Connell suffered a severe injury when he fell in his house, Thunder Rumble was sent to California, with the training duties being over by Chris Speckart. After four starts out of the money, he returned to New York, with O'Connell resuming training duties. On July 20, he prepped for the 1994 Saratoga season by winning a 7-furlong allowance race at Belmont Park. His next stop on his comeback was the $250,000 9-furlong Saratoga Cup Handicap. He went off at 3-1 against Colonial Affair, winner of that year's Belmont Stakes (gr.1); 1993 Jockey Club Gold Cup (gr.1) winner Miner's Mark; 1993 and 1994 Donn Handicap (gr.1) winner Pistols and Roses; 1993 Nassau County Handicap (gr.1) winner West by West; and 1993 Louisiana Super Derby (gr.1) winner

Thunder Rumble, Herb McCauley up, in the lead near the finish line, with Dixie Brass in second, in the 1992 Jim Dandy. *Michele Williams.*

Thunder Rumble, Herb McCauley up, in the post parade prior to the 1992 Travers. *Michele Williams.*

Wallenda. With Richard Migliore in the irons, he settled into second behind the pace-setting Itaka, collared that opponent at the eighth pole and won by 4 lengths. The Saratoga magic eluded him when he ran in the Whitney Stakes (gr.1) against most of the opponents he had beaten in the Saratoga Cup, plus Devil His Due, whom he had defeated two years before in the Travers. He finished fifth, but after the race, it was discovered that he had suffered a ligament injury in his left foreleg, which led to his retirement.

SARATOGA DEW f. (1989; CORMORANT—SUPER LUNA, BY IN REALITY)

Breeder: Penny Chenery
Owners: Sam Huff, Carol Holden and Charles Engel
Trainer: Gary Sciacca
Jockey: Chris Antley
Career Statistics: 11 starts, 8 firsts, 1 second, $541,580

Although her career was relatively short, Saratoga Dew was one of the best New York–bred fillies to set foot on a racetrack. She only raced one year, her 3-year-old season, but was impressive enough to win the Eclipse Award for 3-year-old fillies. She began 1992 by winning two New York–bred races and the listed Over All Stakes by a total of 21 lengths. It was after the latter that Charles Engel bought out his other partners. Her first-class test came in the one-mile Comely Stakes (gr.2) at Aqueduct. She justified her 4-5 odds by winning by 1 length despite being in tight quarters for most of the race. She stretched her winning streak to five when she won the restricted Hyde Park Handicap by a neck. The streak ended when she ran an inexplicably bad race in the one-mile, seventy-yards Post-Deb Stakes (gr.2) at Monmouth Park, finishing sixth as the 5-2 second choice. She rebounded by winning the New York Oaks at Finger Lakes by 8½ lengths as the 2-5 favorite.

It was time to test her mettle against elite company. On August 15, she ran in the historic Alabama Stakes (gr.1) at Saratoga at odds of 6-1. The favorite at 3-2 was California invader Pacific Squall, who had previously won the Hollywood Oaks (gr.1); the second favorite at 2-1 was H. Allen Jerkens's trainee November Snow, winner of the Test two weeks earlier, and the third favorite at 3-1 was Easy Now, second-place finisher in the Mother

Saratoga Dew, Herb McCauley up, in the lead before finishing second to November Snow (no. 3) in the 1992 Alabama. *Michele Williams.*

Goose (gr. 1) and Coaching Club American Oaks (gr. 1) and winner of the Go for Wand Stakes (gr. 1). November Snow won by a nose over Saratoga Dew, with Pacific Squall third, 1¾ lengths behind, and Easy Now seventh and last. After the Alabama, she won the 1⅛-mile Gazelle Stakes (gr. 1) on October 10 by 1¼ lengths, and on October 10, she won the Beldame Stakes (gr. 1) at 2-1 by 6 lengths over the 3-5 favorite Versailles Treaty, a 4-year-old who had previously won the Molly Pitcher Handicap (gr. 2) and the Ruffian Stakes (gr. 1).

The stage was set for the most important race of her career, the 1992 Breeders' Cup Distaff (gr. 1) for fillies and mares 3-years-old and up at Gulfstream Park. The *Blood-Horse* stated that "never in its previous eight runnings...had quality run so deep."[22] Leading her opposition was Paseana, a future National Hall of Fame inductee who had won five Grade 1 races that year, and Versailles Treaty, winner of four Grade 1 races in 1991 and 1992 as well as second to Dance Smartly in the 1991 Distaff, whom Saratoga Dew had beaten handily in her previous race. The bettors made Saratoga Dew the favorite at 2-1, with Paseana and her entrymate Exchange at 5-2 and Versailles Treaty at 7-2. Other notables in the fourteen-horse field included Lite Light, Meadow Star, Fowda and the New York–bred Shared Interest. As expected, Saratoga Dew took the early lead, but Paseana took over near the stretch, winning by 4 lengths over Versailles Treaty. Saratoga Dew tired badly, finishing twelfth. Sensing something wrong, Gary Sciacca

Saratoga Dew, Herb McCauley up, nearing the finish line in the 1992 Beldame *Michele Williams.*

rushed to the finish line and discovered that his filly had grabbed a quarter during the race and had blood streaming profusely from her heel.

The Eclipse Award voters named Saratoga Dew the champion 3-year-old filly for 1992, the first New York–bred to win an Eclipse award (in 1969, New York–bred Silent Screen was voted the best 2-year-old male of that year; the Eclipse Awards were begun in 1971). On the other hand, the *Daily Racing Form* assessed her 121 pounds in the Free Handicap for 3-year-old fillies, 2 less than November Snow and 1 less than Jolypha and Turn Back the Alarm, none of whom ran in the Distaff.

Saratoga Dew was prepping for the 1993 season at Middleburg Training Center in Virginia when she suffered an unspecified career-ending injury. After three years as a broodmare in the United States, she was sent to Japan, where she remained until her retirement.

Chapter 3

HORSES BORN 1990–1999

A in Sociology c. (1990; Ends Well—Social Class, by What a Pleasure)

Breeder: R.I.C. Stable (Prentis Hallenbeck)
Owner: Frederick Rona
Trainer: Phil Johnson
Jockey: no main jockey
Career Statistics: 25 starts, 7 wins, 4 seconds, 4 thirds, $357,856

Winless in three starts in 1992, A in Sociology broke his maiden on May 20, 1993, in a New York–bred turf race at Belmont Park. On August 5, he won the National Museum of Racing and Hall of Fame Stakes (gr.2T) at Saratoga at odds of 15-1, followed by a sixth in the Secretariat (gr.1T) at Arlington Park and a fourth in the Kelso Handicap (gr.3T) at Belmont Park. A in Sociology had 1993 earnings of $134,780.

The year 1994 was his best season, with wins in the Daryl's Joy Handicap (gr.3T) at Saratoga, the second division of the Jaipur Stakes (gr.3T) and the Budweiser Breeders' Cup Handicap (gr.3T) at Belmont. The latter featured a New York–bred exacta, with Fourstars Allstar finishing second. He also finished third in the Kelso Handicap (gr.3T) behind Nijinsky's Secret and Lure. His earnings in 1994 were $201,435. After losing his first four starts in 1995, he was retired.

LOTTSA TALC F. (1990; TALC—ANTILASSA, BY ANTICIPATION)

Breeders/Owners: K.C.W. Stable, Charles Werner, Victor McGuire and Konrad Eggert (died in the fall of 1994)
Trainer: Timothy Kelly
Jockey: no main jockey
Career Statistics: 65 starts, 21 wins, 10 seconds, 12 thirds, $1,206,248

Lottsa Talc was a durable sprinter who never won a race over a mile, won on fast and off tracks and was consistent, finishing in the money in 60 percent of her starts. Winless in her first and last seasons, from 1993 through 1996 she earned $127,100, $159,938, $416,440 and $445,338.

She won her first stakes, the Schenectady Handicap for New York–breds on November 7, 1993, also winning that same race in 1994 and 1995. She took her first graded stakes, the Interborough Breeders' Cup Handicap (gr.3) at Aqueduct, on October 19, 1995, followed by a win in the Berlo Handicap on a muddy Aqueduct track. On February 17, 1996, she won the Barbara Fritchie Handicap (gr.2) at Laurel, followed by another Grade 2 win in the Distaff Handicap at Aqueduct. Her last open stakes victory occurred on September 13, 1996, in the Floral Park at Belmont, followed by her last stakes wins of her career in the Schenectady and Iroquois Handicaps, both for New York–breds. In summary, "Lottsa Talc had class in balance with her courage and quickness. She was a mare with plenty of athletic ability who knew where to find the finish line."[23]

L'CARRIERE G. (1991; CARR DE NASKRA—NORTHERN SUNSET, BY NORTHFIELDS)

Breeder/Owner: Virginia Kraft Payson
Trainers: Roger Attfield and James Bond
Jockey: no primary jockey
Career Statistics: 23 starts, 8 wins, 4 seconds, 3 thirds; $1,726,175

Unraced at two, L'Carriere started ten times in 1994, winning four times at tracks in Maryland, New York and Florida. He participated in no-added-money events and earned $51,835. Before the beginning of his 4-year-old season, his owner made two significant changes. Future National Hall of Fame inductee Roger Attfield was replaced as his trainer by James Bond, who had previously trained Mrs. Payson's horses at Finger Lakes Race Track. The second change was to geld L'Carriere. Whether it was his new trainer, his equipment change, maturity or a combination of the three, L'Carriere went from being a nondescript New York–bred to a force to be reckoned with in the handicap division.

He began his 4-year-old season by winning two allowance races and losing by a nose in the restricted Evan Shipman Handicap. On August 5, he finished second at odds of 10-1 in the Whitney Handicap (gr.1) at Saratoga, 1¾ lengths behind Unaccounted For, who had won the previous year's Jim Dandy Stakes (gr.2). Three weeks later, he met Unaccounted For again in the $250,000 Saratoga Handicap, this time winning by 7 lengths at odds of 3-1. After one month off, L'Carriere finished fourth in the Meadowlands Cup (gr.1) at odds of 2-1 to Peaks and Valleys.

L'Carriere ended his 1995 season with the best and most lucrative performance of his career, finishing second in the Breeders' Cup Classic (gr.1) at odds of 51-1, 2½ lengths behind the 7-10 favorite and future National Hall of Fame inductee Cigar. Behind him were such notables as

L'Carriere, Jorge Chavez in the irons, warming up prior to the 1996 Whitney Handicap. *Michele Williams.*

his old foe Unaccounted For, third, 5-1; Soul of the Matter, fourth, 11-1; Peaks and Valleys, sixth, 15-1; Tinners Way, seventh, 19-1; and Concern, eighth, 19-1. In addition to earning $650,000, with an additional $50,000 from the New York State Breeders' Fund, the race established him as among the best handicap horses in the country not named Cigar. His earnings for 1995 were $928,840.

He began 1996 by losing his first four races, including the Grade 1 Gulfstream Park, Suburban and Whitney Handicaps. Although he finished third to Cigar and Soul of the Matter in the Dubai World Cup, the defeat still netted him $400,000. His only win that year came in his second straight Saratoga Handicap (gr.3). He ended his career on September 14 by finishing second in the Woodward Stakes (gr.1), 4 lengths behind Cigar. His earnings amounted to $745,500, and his total earnings of $1,726,175 established a new record for New York–breds.

DANCIN RENEE F. (1992; DISTINCTIVE PRO—LOLLI LUCKA LOLLI, BY SWEET CANDY)

Breeder/Owner: Sanford Bacon
Trainer: Robert Triola
Jockeys: Richard Migliore and Mike Luzzi
Career Statistics: 21 starts, 14 wins, 5 thirds, $490,258

Dancin Renee, a half sister to the popular Say Florida Sandy, was unraced at two. She won six of ten starts in 1995 and 1996, including the Stallion Stakes, before she had her breakout year in 1997. She began by winning one of her first four starts, the Berlo on Aqueduct's inner dirt track, as well as a seventh in the Barbara Fritchie Handicap (gr.2) at Laurel Park and a fourth in the Correction Handicap at Aqueduct. She then ended her career with seven straight wins, including the Broadway for New York–breds, the Endine at Delaware Park, the $100,000 Straight Deal Breeders' Cup Handicap at Laurel, the Honorable Miss Handicap (gr.3) at Saratoga and the Regret at Monmouth, all in her usual gate-to-wire fashion. She then retired to take up a successful career as a broodmare.

PERFECT ARC F. (1992; BROWN ARC—PODEICA, BY PETRONSKI)

Breeder: Delhanty Stock Farm (Frank Stella)
Owner: Brazil StableB (Paul Sorren)
Trainer: Angel Penna Jr.
Jockey: John Velazquez
Career Statistics: 13 starts, 10 wins, 1 second, 1 third, $668,230

Perfect Arc had an inauspicious 2-year-old season, winning one out of two New York–bred maiden special weight races before being sent to the sidelines for the rest of the year with bucked shins. She began her 3-year-old season by winning an allowance race on the turf, ensuring that she would never run on dirt for the rest of her career. After winning three consecutive races, two of which were listed stakes, she won the 1⅛-mile Diana Handicap (gr.2T) at Saratoga in her usual front-running style against eight fillies and mares as the 3-1 second choice. On September 2, she stretched her winning streak to seven by taking the Rare Perfume Handicap (gr.2T) for 3-year-old fillies at Belmont Park by 2½ lengths as the 4-5 favorite. Finishing second was the Del Mar Oaks (gr.1T) winner Bail Out Becky. She ended her season by winning the prestigious Queen Elizabeth II Cup (gr.1T) at 1⅛ miles as the 7-10 favorite. Penna opted against sending her to California to compete against older turf horses, ending her season with a perfect seven-for-seven record with earnings of $449,150.

Perfect Arc's 4-year-old season was a disappointment, even taking into consideration that it is hard to top a perfect record. She began by extending her unbeaten streak to nine, eight on the turf, when she won an allowance race at Belmont Park. Her streak ended on July 24 when she finished fourth by 1¼ lengths as the 4-5 favorite in the Matchmaker Stakes (gr.2T) at Atlantic City. She also lost her next race, the 1³⁄₁₆-mile Beverly D. Stakes (gr.2T) at Arlington Park, finishing second to the Irish-bred Timarida by 2½ lengths. The winner, whom Marty McGee described as "one of the world's premier turf fillies,"[24] was the 3-2 favorite with her entrymate Khalisa, while Perfect Arc was the 4-1 second choice. She ended her season, and her career, by taking the Noble Damsel Handicap (gr.3T) as the 2-5 favorite.

VICTORY SPEECH C. (1993; DEPUTY MINISTER—IDA'S IMAGE, BY ALYDAR)

Breeder: Robert Entenmann
Owners: Robert Entenmann; Michael Tabor and Mrs. John Magnier
Trainers: Robert Triola; D. Wayne Lukas
Jockey: no main jockey
Career Statistics: 27 starts, 9 firsts, 2 seconds, 5 thirds, $1,289,020

Victory Speech began his career under the ownership of his breeder, Robert Entenmann. After he broke his maiden in his second start of his 2-year-old season, he was scheduled to make his stakes debut in the Tremont (gr.3) on June 28 at Belmont Park. The day before the race, he was purchased in a private sale by Michael Tabor and Mrs. John Magnier. No doubt Tabor was hoping lightning would strike twice, since in November 1994 he had purchased a 2-year-old horse named Thunder Gulch who went on to win the 1995 Kentucky Derby. Victory Speech finished third in the Tremont and didn't race again until October, when he finished third in an allowance race. He then won three straight allowance races, the last by 11½ lengths on February 4, 1996, at Gulfstream Park.

He continued the 1996 season on February 24 in the Fountain of Youth Stakes (gr.2), finishing third at 6-1, 1½ lengths behind the 143-1 winner Built for Pleasure, who was a neck ahead of the 4-5 favorite Unbridled's Song, winner of the 1995 Breeders' Cup Juvenile. Finishing fifth was the 2-1 second choice Editor's Note, who would win that year's Belmont (gr.1). The next stop was Turfway Park and the $600,000 Jim Beam Stakes (gr.2), where he was made the 9-10 favorite. However, he disappointed the bettors and his handlers by finishing third, 5½ lengths behind the winner, the 5-2 second choice Roar.

Undeterred, Lukas sent him to Louisville for the Kentucky Derby. Victory Speech and his stablemate Honour and Glory both ran in the navy blue and orange colors of last year's winner Thunder Gulch, but that was the only thing either colt had in common with the 1995 3-year-old champion, as Victory Speech finished tenth and Honour and Glory eighteenth at 24-1. The winner was Grindstone, with the 7-2 favorite Unbridled's Song finishing fifth. Finishing twelfth was Skip Away, who be Victory Speech's nemesis for the next two years.

The day after the Derby, Lukas stated that Victory Speech would not go to the Preakness Stakes (gr.1), but he did enter him at the last minute. He finished fifth at 40-1, 10 lengths behind the winner Louis Quatorze. Finishing second was Skip Away, the first of many races that Victory Speech would trail the future National Hall of Fame inductee.

Victory Speech's next race was the Ohio Derby (gr.2) at Thistledown, finishing second to Skip Away. On July 6, he won his first graded stakes, taking the Dwyer (gr.2) at Belmont Park as the 9-10 favorite against moderate opposition. Two weeks later, he went west and won his second stakes in a row, taking the Swaps (gr.2) at Hollywood Park as the 4-5 favorite and setting a stakes record of 1:48 1/5 set the previous year by Thunder Gulch. Returning east, Victory Speech lost two more races to Skip Away, finishing third, 2 lengths behind him in the Haskell Invitational (gr.1) at Monmouth Park, and sixth, 8¾ lengths behind in the Woodbine Million (gr.1). On October 4, he finished ninth, 18 lengths behind Dramatic Gold in the Meadowlands Cup (gr.1). Two weeks later he, was given a confidence boost when he won the New York–bred Empire Classic by ¾ of a length. He finished the year in California, winning the Laz Barrera Handicap (gr.3) as the 4-5 favorite and finishing sixth as the even-money favorite in the Malibu Stakes (gr.1) at Santa Anita, the first leg of the Strub Series. Although Victory Speech did not win the Kentucky Derby for Mr. Tabor, his $869,260 in earnings for the year should have provided some solace.

Victory Speech began 1997 the same as he ended 1996, losing a leg of the Strub Series as the favorite, this time finishing sixth in the San Fernando Breeders' Cup to Northern Afleet. On February 2, he confounded the bettors by winning the third leg, the Strub (gr.1), at odds of 7-1. After the Strub, he returned east to finish his career in one long nightmare. He finished out of the money in the Gulfstream Park Handicap (gr.1), the Oaklawn Handicap (gr.1), the Excelsior Breeders' Cup Handicap (gr.2), the Stephen Foster Handicap (gr.2) and, most stunning of all, the Empire Classic Handicap, by a combined total of 63 lengths. None of those losses was to Skip Away. However, mostly because of his win in the Strub, he still managed to win $365,198 from only one win in seven starts.

Say Florida Sandy c. (1994; Personal Flag—Lolli Lucka Lolli, by Sweet Candy)

Breeder: Sanford Bacon
Owners: Sanford Bacon; Jane E. Marinos; John Rotello
Trainers: Robert Triola; Gasper Moschera; Juan Serey; Jose Serrano; Scott Lake
Jockey: no primary jockey
Career Statistics: 98 starts, 33 wins, 17 seconds, 12 thirds, $2,085,408

Say Florida Sandy was one of the most popular and durable New York–breds in history. His breeder and original owner, Sanford Bacon, also owned and bred his older half sister, Dancin Renee. As a 2-year-old, he won four of eight starts, taking the restricted Aspirant and New York Breeders' Futurity at Finger Lakes and, in his last race of the year, the New York State Great White Way. He also finished second in the Tremont Stakes (gr.3) and third in the Sanford Stakes (gr.3) to Kelly Kip, who would become a star sprinter for trainer H. Allen Jerkens. Significantly, the only time he finished out of the money was in the 9-furlong Moet Champagne (gr.1) at Saratoga, when he finished ninth, giving an indication that, like his half sister, he was strictly a sprinter. His earnings in 1996 came to $235,720.

His 1997 season was the worst of his eight-year career, earning only $79,140 from eleven starts. His fortunes did not improve after he was claimed by Gasper Moschera on September 14 for $70,000 on behalf of Jane Marinos. Seven races later, on February 22, 1998, he was claimed by Juan Serey for John Rotella for $60,000. That claim turned out to be a lucrative one, as he won numerous stakes wins during his remaining six years. After winning two allowance races for his new connections, he finished second in the Bold Ruler (gr.3), 6 lengths behind Kelly Kip. He rebounded from that loss by winning his first open stakes, the Wilmington Handicap at Delaware Park, as the 2-1 second choice. After losing three races, including a fourth in the Finger Lakes Breeders' Cup to Kelly Kip and Affirmed Success, he won three in a row, taking the Shrewsbury at Monmouth Park, a handicap at Belmont Park and the Teddy Drone at Monmouth Park as the 6-5 favorite. After his streak was snapped by a second in the Longfellow at Monmouth Park, he lost four of his next five races. He ended his season by winning his first graded stakes, taking the Gravesend Handicap (gr.3) at Aqueduct on December 26. His total earnings for 1998 were $395,151, impressive considering he was claimed for $60,000.

The year 1999 was an off-season, with two wins from nine starts, with no stakes victories. As he did in 1998, he rebounded from a mediocre season to have a lucrative one in 2000. He started slowly, losing his first three starts, but he won three of his next four races, including his second Shrewsbury at Monmouth Park. After finishing second in the Philadelphia Breeders' Cup Handicap (gr.3) and third in the Longfellow Stakes to the multi-stakes winning sprinter Delaware Township, he won his second General Douglas McArthur Handicap for New York–breds at Belmont Park. He ended his season with his second win in the Gravesend Handicap (gr.3), giving him earnings of $366,787.

Like good wine, Say Florida Sandy got better as he got older. Remarkably, he had his best year as a 7-year-old in 2001, with graded stakes wins in the Bold Ruler Handicap (gr.3), with Delaware Township second; the True North Handicap (gr.2); and Philadelphia Breeders' Cup Handicap (gr.3). He also finished second to Peeping Tom in the Carter Handicap (gr.1) and lost by a head to Exchange Rate in the Tom Fool Handicap (gr.2). Ungraded stakes wins were in the Hollie Hughes Handicap for New York–breds and the Paterson Handicap at the Meadowlands. After the Paterson, he lost his last five races of the season, including a third in the DeFrancis Memorial (gr.1) at Laurel. Despite his late season slump, he still managed to earn $615,420, the most in his career.

Although he earned $216,262 in 2002, none of his three wins in twelve starts came in stakes races. His best performance that season occurred on August 11 at Saratoga, where he finished second, 2 lengths behind that year's sprint champion, Orientate, in the Alfred G. Vanderbilt Handicap (gr.2). Earlier that year, he finished fourth in the Carter Handicap (gr.1), 3 lengths behind the multi–Grade 1 stakes sprinter Affirmed Success. In 2003, his last year of racing, he started six times, with one of his two wins coming in the Paumonok Handicap by disqualification. He still managed to win $96,602 as a 9-year-old.

After he retired, he stood at stud at Buckridge Farm near Kinderhook, New York, before retiring to Old Friends in Kentucky.

INCURABLE OPTIMIST c. (1996; CURE THE BLUES—MISS TURLINGTON, BY SEATTLE SLEW)

Breeders: Dr. William B. Wilmot and Dr. Joan M. Taylor
Owners: John T. Behrendt and Theresa E. Behrendt
Trainer: David Donk
Jockey: John Velazquez
Career Statistics: 6 starts, 4 wins, 1 second, 1 third, $271,310

Incurable Optimist was headed for a possible Eclipse Award when his career was cut short by an injury. He lost his first two races as a 2-year-old, both New York–bred maiden races on the dirt. On August 11 at Saratoga, he won an open maiden special weight on the turf by 14 lengths as the 3-2 favorite. After his maiden win, he took three turf stakes in a row: the World Appeal at the Meadowlands at odds of 9-10, the Pilgrim (gr.3T) at Belmont Park at 1-2 and the Generous (gr.3T) at Hollywood Park at 1-2, winning by 9 lengths. After his win in the Generous, the *Blood-Horse* could hardly contain its enthusiasm: "The competition has no remedy, no cure, for his devastating control of the race....Incurable Optimist is one of those young colts that make racing on the turf look like a canter through the park."[25] He was scheduled for a forty-five-day vacation after his win at Hollywood Park, but a tendon injury ended what undoubtedly would have been a brilliant career.

In a conversation with David Donk during the 2018 Saratoga meet, Donk called Incurable Optimist the most talented horse he had ever trained. After doing some research, I saw him again the next day and asked how Incurable Optimist compared to Awad, an earlier Donk trainee who had won four Grade 1 races on the turf, with earnings of $3,270,131. Donk replied that "Awad was the most accomplished, but Incurable Optimist was the most talented." High praise indeed.

BELLE CHERIE F. (1996; BELONG TO ME—BELLE NUIT, BY DR. CARTER)

Breeders: Belle Meadow Farm (Jeffrey Foong) and Amherst Stable (Phil Johnson and family)
Owners: Jeffrey Foong and Phil Johnson; Lael Stable (Roy and Gretchen Jackson)
Trainer: Phil Johnson
Jockey: John Velazquez
Career Statistics: 19 starts, 6 wins, 1 third, $426,861

Belle Cherie won three of her four starts as a 2-year-old and finished her year with a win in the Miss Grillo Stakes (gr.3T). Eight days before that race, Phil Johnson sold his share in the filly to Roy and Gretchen Jackson's Lael Stable, with Johnson continuing as the filly's trainer.

What looked like a promising career on the turf changed course when she lost her first three races of her 3-year-old season, finishing fourth in the Sands Point (gr.3T) and the restricted Mount Vernon Handicap at odds of 2-1 and 4-5, respectively, and fifth in the Lake George (gr.3T) at Saratoga. Following the Lake George, Johnson felt that a change of surface was called for, and on September 6, she won the $1\frac{1}{16}$-mile Honey Bee Handicap (gr.3) on the dirt at the Meadowlands at odds of 26-1. In her next start, she finished fourth, in the $1\frac{1}{16}$-mile Cotillion Handicap (gr.2) at Philadelphia Park, followed by consecutive wins in the $1\frac{1}{8}$-mile Turnback the Alarm (gr.3) at Aqueduct and the 1-mile Top Flight Handicap (gr.2) at Aqueduct by 7 lengths at odds of 5-1. She ended her season with a fourth in the 1¼-mile Ladies Handicap as the favorite at odds of 4-5, giving her a season's earnings of $277,899. After going winless in seven starts in 2000, she was retired.

GANDER G. (1996; CORMORANT—LOVELY NURSE, BY SAWBONES)

Breeder: Angela Rugnetta
Owners: Mike Gatsas and Ted Gatsas
Trainers: Charles Assapoulos; John P. Terranova II
Jockeys: John Velazquez; Sean Bridgmohan
Career Statistics: 60 starts, 15 wins, 10 seconds, 9 thirds, $1,824,011

In 1998 and 1999, the gray, almost white gelding Gander amassed winnings of $700,338, most of which was earned in allowances and handicaps, as well as placing in the 1999 restricted Damon Runyan and finishing third in the Paterson at the Meadowlands. On September 18, 1999, he was entered in his first graded event, the Woodward Stakes (gr.1), finishing fifth, at odds of 37-1, 6 lengths behind the winner, River Keen. In later years, the Woodward would be the scene of some of his finest efforts. On October 2, he won the Empire Classic Handicap for New York–breds by a neck as the 2-1 favorite.

At the end of his 3-year-old season, Gander resembled a solid horse who would return a nice annual profit for his owners by competing in lucrative New York–bred races and ungraded stakes events. This assessment took a nosedive when he opened his 2000 season by finishing fifth in an open allowance, followed by an eighth, 10 lengths back in the restricted Kings Point Handicap at odds of 7-2. After two allowance wins, he was once again found wanting in graded stakes, finishing fifth in the Massachusetts Handicap (gr.2) at Suffolk Downs to the popular international traveler Running Stag. Although his Massachusetts Handicap could be excused, his next race would be the nadir of his career, finishing fifth, 25 lengths back in an open allowance at Belmont at odds of 3-2.

Inexplicably, Gander's form took a radical 180-degree turn for the better. On July 23, he began his resurgence when he won the restricted Evan Shipman Handicap at Belmont Park at odds of 7-1. In his next race, he took third in the Saratoga Breeders' Cup Handicap (gr.2), and on September

16, he finished third, ¾ of a length behind handicap stars Lemon Drop Kid, winner of that year's Grade 1 Pimlico Special and Whitney, and Behrens in the Woodward Stakes (gr.1) at odds of 41-1. One month later, he once more took on the best handicap horses on the East Coast, finishing second, 6 lengths behind Albert the Great in the Jockey Club Gold Cup (gr.1). Finishing behind him were Lemon Drop Kid (fifth) and Behrens (sixth). In accordance with the weight-for-age conditions of the Gold Cup, all horses carried 126 pounds except for the 3-year-old Albert the Great, who carried 122. Gander ended his 2000 season with a ninth in the Breeders' Cup Classic (gr.1) at Churchill Downs. His 2000 earnings were $388,290. After the season was over, Mr. Assapoulos graciously argued that Gander needed a trainer who was based in New York State, and the Gatsas brothers turned the reins over to John Terranova, who would be his trainer for the remainder of Gander's career.

Gander's assault on the top handicap horses in the East went in reverse when he opened his 2001 season by finishing third in the Donn Handicap (gr.1) at odds of 13-1, 11 lengths behind Captain Steve and Albert the Great, and fifth in the Gulfstream Park Handicap (gr.1). After an allowance win at Belmont Park, he continued his string of disappointing performances in graded stakes when he finished fourth in the Brooklyn Handicap (gr.2), almost 7 lengths behind Albert the Great at odds of 6-1. Although he finished second, 7 lengths behind Hap in the New Hampshire Sweepstakes (gr.3) at Rockingham Park, he only went off at 5-2.

On July 28, he regained some of his lost prestige when he finished third, 2¼ lengths behind Lido Palace and Albert the Great in the Whitney Stakes (gr.1) at odds of 35-1. After he finished a disappointing fourth in the Saratoga Breeders' Cup Handicap to Aptitude, on September 28 he won his only graded stakes when he took the Meadowlands Cup Handicap (gr.2) at odds of 4-1, with Include finishing third. He ended the season with a ninth in the Breeders' Cup Classic (gr.1) at Belmont Park and a fifth in the Clark Handicap (gr.2) at Churchill Downs, only 2 lengths behind the first two finishers, Ubiquity and Include. In 2001, he managed to win the most money in his career, $557,060, with $300,000 coming from the Meadowlands Cup.

On February 3, Gander began his 2002 season on the West Coast, finishing seventh in the San Antonio Handicap (gr.2) at Santa Anita. He returned home, and on April 2, he lost by a nose in the Kings Point for New York–breds at odds of 3-4, followed by a third and a first in two allowances. On August 17, he ran in the Saratoga Breeders' Cup Handicap at odds of

12-1. Shortly after leaving the gate, he dumped his jockey, Mike Smith, and engaged with the leaders the entire race. Always a favorite at Saratoga, the roar of the crowd as he neared the finish line urged him on. Although he was nosed out by Evening Attire, many observers sensed that Gander thought he had won the race, and there was nobody to contradict him.

On September 7, he ran another spectacular race in the Woodward Stakes (gr.1), similar to his great effort in the 2000 edition against Lemon Drop Kid and Behrens. In the 2002 race, his main opponents were Lido Palace, winner of the 2001 Whitney and Woodward, and Express Tour. The three raced to the finish line as a team, with Lido Palace beating Gander for first by half a length, who in turn nosed out Express Tour for second. The 2002 Woodward would be the last time Gander would compete on equal terms with standout handicap horses. He ended the year with earnings of $306,000.

During his last two years of racing, Gander won three of twelve races, with combined earnings of $200,323. While he was a profitable horse, his days of running against the likes of Albert the Great and Lemon Drop Kid were over. On August 31, 2004, he suffered a career-ending injury while working out at Saratoga. Fortunately, he was able to be saved, and he is presently living a well-earned life of leisure at Stone Bridge Farm in Saratoga County. Although purists might sniff that Gander's fifteen lifetime wins only included one graded stakes, his many fans would be quick to point out that his efforts in such Grade 1 events as the 2000 and 2002 Woodward Stakes, the 2000 Jockey Club Gold Cup and the 2000 Whitney Stakes more than atoned for the lack of a Grade 1 win on his résumé.

CRITICAL EYE F. (1997; DYNAFORMER—CRITICAL CREW, BY DR. BLUM)

Breeder: Herbert Schwartz
Owners: Herbert Schwartz and Carol A. Schwartz
Trainer: Scott Schwartz
Jockeys: Mike Luzzi, Jorge Chavez and C.C. Lopez
Career Statistics: 28 starts, 14 wins, 4 seconds, 3 thirds, $1,066,984

Critical Eye, who was trained by the owners' son Scott, did not begin to show her true ability until the summer of her 3-year-old season. Of her first twelve starts, her only stakes race was the listed Christiana on the turf at Delaware Park, finishing seventh. Most of her other starts were in New York–bred allowance races, and showing her versatility, three of those races were on the turf, with two wins.

Her period of profitable mediocrity came to a halt on July 31, 2000, at Saratoga when she finished first in an open allowance race on a sloppy track in which she was sent off at odds of 7-1. On August 19, she finished fourth in the historic Alabama Stakes (gr.1) at Saratoga, 5 lengths behind the winner Jostle. She outraced her odds of 47-1, against a stellar field that included the winner (3-1), who had previously won the Black-Eyed Susan (gr.2) and the Coaching Club American Oaks (gr.1); Secret Status, second, the 9-10 favorite, who had previously won the Kentucky Oaks (gr.1) and Mother Goose (gr.1); and Spain, third, 7-1, who had previously won the La Brea Stakes (gr.1) at Santa Anita and would later win that year's Breeders' Cup Distaff (gr.1).

Following the Alabama, she established herself as one of the better fillies on the East Coast when she won the Gazelle Handicap (gr.1) at Belmont Park at odds of 24-1. Scott Schwartz remarked on her versatility, "This filly has really developed into something special. She can sprint, go long, run on the dirt and run on the grass."[26] Critical Eye also won her next race, the Honey Bee Handicap (gr.3) at the Meadowlands, as the 3-2 favorite. She ended her 3-year-old season by losing the New York–bred Ticonderoga Handicap by a neck on the turf and finishing third in the Top Flight Handicap (gr.3) at Aqueduct at odds of 7-2. Her late surge resulted in earnings of $457,730 for the season.

She had two graded stakes wins in 2001, the first in the 1⅜-mile Sheepshead Bay Handicap (gr.2T), which was moved to a muddy main track at Aqueduct, thus accounting for her even-money odds and winning margin of 7½ lengths. The second was an impressive victory in the 1⅛-mile Hempstead Handicap (gr.1) at Belmont Park at odds of 11-1. Finishing second was her old foe Jostle at 5-2, and seventh and last was the 3-4 favorite Beautiful Pleasure, a multi-Grade-1-winning 6-year-old who was returning from surgery for colic. Critical Eye's only other graded stakes in the money was a second in the Bed o' Roses Handicap (gr.3), losing by a nose to Country Hideaway. After the Hempstead, she ended her season out of the money in four Grade 1 events: the Go for Wand Handicap, sixth at 3-5; the Personal Ensign Handicap, seventh, 26½ lengths behind at 5-1; the Beldame, fourth at 23-1; and the Breeders' Cup Distaff, eighth at 36-1. Her earnings were still a healthy $339,736.

In 2002, her only graded stakes win was in the Ladies Handicap (gr.3) at Aqueduct. She finished with earnings of $229,071 from twelve starts. After her retirement, the New York Racing Association named a race after her, a $200,000 stakes at one mile on the dirt for New York–bred fillies.

WHITMORE'S CONN C. (1998; KRIS S.—ALBONITA, BY DEPUTED TESTAMONY)

Breeders: Bud Wolf and Joe D'Agostino
Owners: Michael Shanley and Lynn Shanley
Trainer: Scotty Schulhofer
Jockeys: Edgar Prado; Sean Bridgmohan
Career Statistics: 28 starts, 7 wins, 4 seconds, 5 thirds, $740,426

Whitmore's Conn was another late bloomer. Although Scotty Schulhofer was listed as his official trainer, his son Randy Schulhofer was his actual trainer for all his four years of racing. His first two years produced only two wins from thirteen starts, none of them in stakes, with earnings of over $126,000. Although he had some success on the dirt, it was obvious halfway through his sophomore season that grass was his preferred surface. He made his graded stakes debut on June 16, 2001, at Belmont Park, finishing sixth in the 10-furlong Hill Prince (gr.3T) at odds of 22-1, followed by a third in the Lexington (gr.3T). After a fifth in the Albany and third in the Ashley T. Cole, both restricted to New York–breds on the dirt, he stayed on the turf for the rest of his career. He ended his 2002 season with a third in the Lawrence Realization (gr.3T) and eighth in a restricted allowance.

After winning two of his first four starts in 2002 in allowance events and finishing sixth in the Kingston Handicap for New York–breds on July 13, he won the 1¾-mile Bowling Green Handicap (gr.2T) at Belmont Park. He followed that win by losing the last four races of the year, including a sixth, only 3¼ lengths behind With Anticipation in the 1½-mile Sword Dancer Handicap (gr.1T) at Saratoga, with Denon second, and a fifth in the 1½-mile Turf Classic (gr.1T) at Belmont Park, 3¼ lengths behind the winner, Denon. His earnings for 2002 were $210,100.

Although his last season of racing would be the most successful of his career, he began 2003 with four straight losses, fifth in the William L. McKnight Handicap (gr.2T) at Calder, 2½ lengths behind the winner, Man

From Wicklow, being the only race of the four in which he was competitive. On July 12, he won his second Bowling Green Handicap (gr.2T), coming from behind in his usual style, at odds of 11-1. His next race was the highlight of his career, taking the Sword Dancer Handicap (gr.1T) at odds of 24-1, with Denon, the 2-1 favorite, finishing fourth. He ended his career with a seventh in the Man o' War Stakes (gr.1T) at odds of 5-1 on a surface described as "yielding and sticky." His earnings for 2003 were $404,236, with $300,000 of that coming from the Sword Dancer. One curious fact from his career was that he won three graded stakes but was winless in five New York–bred stakes, two on the dirt and three on the turf. Shortly after his loss in the Man o' War, the Shanleys announced that Whitmore's Conn was being sent to Ireland to assume stud duties at Bert House in County Kildare.

CARSON HOLLOW F. (1999; CARSON CITY—LIZEALITY, BY HOLD YOUR PEACE)

Breeder: Patricia S. Purdy
Owners: Hemlock Farm (Frank Hemlock), Gabrielle Farm (John and Chip Acierno), Justin Zimmerman; Sanford Goldfarb; Frank Stronach
Trainer: Richard Dutrow Jr.
Jockey: John Velazquez
Career Statistics: 10 starts, 6 wins, 3 seconds, $500,110

Carson Hollow, one of the fastest fillies of her generation, was known more for a Grade 1 race she lost than for the three graded races she won. She was bought by a syndicate as an unraced 2-year-old on the advice of Richard Dutrow Jr., who in turn heard about her from his brother Tony Dutrow, a trainer in Maryland.

After handily winning her first three races in 2002, including the Bouwerie for New York–breds as the 9-10 favorite, she won the Prioress Stakes (gr.1) at Belmont Park in her usual front-running style. Just prior to the Prioress, Frank Stronach bought 60 percent of the filly, with the rest of the original syndicate retaining the other 40 percent.

Her next race was the toughest of the filly's short career, the 7-furlong Test Stakes (gr.1) at Saratoga. Her main opposition was the Bob Frankel–trained You, a former $50,000 claimer who had already won four Grade 1 races. You was the 9-10 favorite, and Carson Hollow was the 5-2 second choice in the seven-horse field. As usual, Carson Hollow jumped out to the lead, with You trapped behind horses. You finally caught up to the frontrunner at the turn for home, but despite setting early fractions of 21.60 and 44.27, Carson Hollow managed to stay with her opponent as they raced to the wire. As described by Steve Haskin, "This was no head-bobbing battle, but two heads moving as one. Many felt they hit the wire dead even, but the photo revealed You's nose in front by the narrowest of margins. Both fillies returned to a rousing ovation from the appreciative Saratoga crowd."[27] It was one of the most thrilling stretch runs seen in recent years at that historic track.

Carson Hollow rebounded from the strenuous Test to win her next race, the Floral Park (gr.3) at Belmont Park as the 1-2 favorite. On October 26, she ended her season on a sour note by finishing last of sixteen horses in the Breeders' Cup Sprint at Arlington Park at odds of 18-1. She was the only 3-year-old filly in the field, which was won by the 3-2 favorite Orientate. Carson Hollow ended her season with earnings of $335,370.

She began her 4-year-old campaign by finishing second to the future National Hall of Fame inductee Xtra Heat in the Barbara Fritchie Handicap (gr.2) on a sloppy track at Laurel Park. She won her next start, the Distaff Breeders' Cup Handicap (gr.2) at Aqueduct, as the 1-2 favorite. On May 11, she ended her career with a disappointing second as the 6-5 favorite to Shine Again in the Genuine Risk Handicap (gr.2) at Belmont Park. After recovering from surgery for the removal of a bone chip, she died on August 25 following complications from colic surgery.

Chapter 4

HORSES BORN 2000–2009

Funny Cide g. (2000; Distorted Humor—Belle's Good Cide, by Slewcide)

Breeder: WinStar Farm
Owner: Sackatoga Stable (Jack Knowlton, Managing Partner; Gus Williams;
*   David Mahan; Lew Tittleton; Eric Dattner; Mark Phillips; Jon Constance; Pete*
*   Phillips; Larry Rheinhardt)*
Trainer: Barclay Tagg
Jockey: Jose Santos
Career Statistics: 38 starts, 11 wins, 6 seconds, 8 thirds, $3,539,412

Rather than members of the landed gentry, Middle East sheiks or Wall Street millionaires who are the usual owners of the Sport of Kings, Sackatoga Stable consisted mainly of high school buddies from Sackett Harbor and Saratoga Springs, New York. They were solid middle-class citizens who probably spent their Saturdays mowing their lawns. After making their original investment in a horse they claimed for $40,000, made $160,000 and was claimed from them for $62,500, they had the wherewithal to buy Funny Cide for the $75,000 asking price. This transaction was completed on the advice of their trainer, Barclay Tagg, who had had his eye on the gelding since he first saw him as a yearling. The man who sold the 2-year-old was its original owner, Tony Everard, who first purchased him for $22,000 at the Fasig-Tipton New York–bred sale at Saratoga. Tagg's high opinion of Funny Cide was justified when he won his first three races in 2002, a maiden special weight and the Bertram F. Bongard and Sleepy Hollow Stakes, all restricted to New York–breds. His season ended prematurely when he developed a chronic lung congestion, leaving him with earnings of $136,185.

Funny Cide's three-race winning streak ended on January 18, 2000, when he finished fifth in the Holy Bull (gr.3) at Gulfstream Park after hitting the gate at the start and fanning four-wide around the first turn. After taking more time off to deal with his lung condition, he started getting noticed by the betting public when he finished second by disqualification in the Louisiana Derby (gr.2) at odds of 6-1, 3½ lengths behind the Bobby Frankel–trained Peace Rules. Funny Cide would have many more opportunities to get better acquainted with that opponent during his 3- and 4-year old seasons. The gelding gained even more credibility on April 12 when he finished second in the Wood Memorial (gr.1) at Aqueduct behind Empire Maker, another Frankel trainee the gelding would see more often in 2003 and 2004. The next time he would meet those to foes would be on the first Saturday in May in Louisville, Kentucky.

On May 3, Funny Cide became the first New York–bred to achieve acclaim of the general public when he won the Kentucky Derby (gr.1) at odds of 12-1. Finishing second was Empire Maker, the favorite at 5-2, and finishing third was Peace Rules, the 6-1 second favorite. Ironically, it was Funny Cide's first graded stakes win. Stalking the leaders to the top of the stretch, he pulled away to win by 1¾ lengths, the first gelding to win the Derby since Clyde Van Dusen in 1929 and the first New York–bred to win it. As Steve Haskin wrote in the *Blood-Horse*, "On May 3, a new chapter was written in the annals of America's greatest horse race, scripted in Frank Capra fashion by a long, lean chestnut gelding with the convivial name of Funny Cide."[28]

Two weeks later, Funny Cide proved that the Derby was no fluke when he won the Preakness Stakes (gr.1) as the 3-2 favorite, stalking the frontrunners as he did two weeks earlier. By the turn for home, he was 5 lengths in front, and when he hit the wire, he had won by 9¾ lengths under a hand ride by Jose Santos. Trailing in fourth was the 2-1 second choice Peace Rules.

On June 7, the fairy tale ended when Funny Cide finished third, 5 lengths behind the winner Empire Maker in the sloppy 1½-mile Belmont

Stakes (gr.1). He was the even-money favorite, as well as the overwhelming sentimental favorite, with the winner the second choice at 2-1. The finish was described by Steve Haskin: "The golden carriage named Funny Cide was not going to change into a pumpkin, as so many others in the past. After a quarter of a century, it was time for fairy tale and reality to cross paths. But then it happened…again."[29]

On August 3, he lost again, finishing third as the even-money favorite in the $1.1 million Haskell Invitational (gr.1) at Monmouth Park. Finishing first, 9 lengths ahead of Funny Cide, was the other Frankel trainee, Peace Rules. He ended his season by finishing ninth in the Breeders' Cup Classic (gr.1) at Santa Anita at odds of 8-1, 14 lengths behind the winner, Pleasantly Perfect.

His three-race losing streak did not prevent Funny Cide from winning the Eclipse Award for 3-year-old males. He was the second New York–bred to win an Eclipse, the first being Saratoga Dew. His 2003 earnings of $1,963,200 were a new record for New York–breds.

After beginning his 4-year-old season with a win in a $100,000 optional claiming race at Gulfstream Park, Funny Cide finished the year by running in nine graded stakes and did well enough to establish himself as one of the better handicap horses in the country. He had two wins in those stakes, the first on April 3 when he took the Excelsior Breeders' Cup Handicap (gr.3) on a muddy Aqueduct track at even money, with Evening Attire finishing second. On October 2, he won the third Grade 1 of his career, taking the mile-and-a-quarter Jockey Club Gold Cup at Belmont Park. When he crossed the finish line, the roar of the 16,864 in attendance was evidence that his popularity had not waned. Regular jockey Jose Santos called Funny Cide's Gold Cup victory "the best race he ever ran."[30] Other finishes in the money came in the Massachusetts Handicap (gr.2), second by a head behind Offlee Wild; a second in the Saratoga Breeders' Cup Handicap (gr.2), 5 lengths behind Evening Attire; a neck behind old foe Peace Rules in the Suburban Handicap (gr.1); and a third in the New Orleans Handicap (gr.2), 5 lengths behind Medaglia d'Oro. He ended the year with another disappointing Breeders' Cup Classic (gr.1) loss, 14 lengths behind Ghostzapper, another Bob Frankel trainee. He ended the year with earnings of $1,075,100.

The year 2006 was a lost one for Funny Cide. After finishing off the board in three events, he was diagnosed with a bad back and was retired for the rest of the year. In 2007, he won one open stakes, the Dominion Day (gr.3) at Woodbine, and he ended the year with earnings of $235,284.

Funny Cide, Jose Santos up, warming up prior to the 2004 Saratoga Breeders' Cup. *Michele Williams.*

In 2008, his last year of racing, he won one race in four starts, the restricted Wadsworth Memorial, before his back problems forced his retirement. For five years, he was a stable pony for Barclay Tagg, but his back problems worsened and he was shipped to Kentucky Horse Park, where he continues to be a fan favorite.

To say that Funny Cide was a popular horse would be a vast understatement. He was the first New York–bred to gain national recognition and gave the New York–bred program a tremendous boost. His feats were instrumental in showing that syndication was a viable way for ordinary fans to get financially involved in horse racing. The "common man" aspect of his owners appealed to the public. Finally, he once more justified Stephen Sanford's faith that a champion Thoroughbred can be bred in New York State.

Friends Lake c. (2001; A.P. Indy—Antespend, by Spend a Buck)

Breeders/Owners: Chester Broman and Mary Broman
Trainer: John Kimmel
Jockey: Richard Migliore
Career Statistics: 7 starts, 3 wins, 1 third, $696,400

After winning two of his three starts at two, including the $100,000 Sleepy Hollow Stakes for New York–breds, Friends Lake began his 3-year-old season by finishing a disappointing third in the Holy Bull (gr.3) at Gulfstream Park at odds of 3-1 after acting up in the paddock and the starting gate. His next race was the Florida Derby (gr.1), with the even-money favorite being the New York–bred Read the Footnotes. Ignored by the bettors, Friends Lake won by ¾ of a length at odds of 37-1. Kimmel had to train Friends Lake up to the Kentucky Derby after the colt sustained an injury, finishing fifteenth, 36 lengths behind the winner, Smarty Jones. After finishing seventh in the Peter Pan (gr.2), he was retired.

Fleet Indian f. (2001; Indian Charlie—Hustleeta, by Afleet)

Breeders: Becky Thomas, Lewis Lakin and Brenda Lakin
Owners: Stan E. Fulton; Paul H. Sayor
Trainers: James Toner; Todd Pletcher
Jockeys: Jose Santos, Edgar Prado and John Velazquez
Career Statistics: 19 starts, 13 wins, 1 third, $1,704,513

Fleet Indian didn't reach her full potential until late in her career. Unraced at two, her first two years of racing were, for the most part, restricted to allowance events. She made her debut in graded stakes company on August 21, 2004, when she finished a distant fifth to Society Selection in the Alabama Stakes (gr.1) at Saratoga. On November 27, 2005, she won the restricted Montauk Handicap by 5 lengths as the 4-5 favorite. She finished the year with an allowance win at Philadelphia, which, combined with the Montauk, was the beginning of an eight-race winning streak. Her combined earnings for her first two years of racing were $140,793 from twelve starts.

In January 2006, she was sold to Atlanta businessman Paul H. Sayor for $290,000 at the Keeneland horses of all ages sale, and the training duties were handed over to Todd Pletcher. They would be her new connections when she became a champion filly. It would be tempting to assume that her heightened status was a direct result of Pletcher taking over the training duties, but such was not the case. After her win in the Sixty Sails, Saylor was quoted as saying that after he acquired her, Fleet Indian's former trainer, Jimmy Toner, advised him, "Don't make her a broodmare. I've just gotten her back to where she needs to run."[31] After her win in the Next Move Handicap, Pletcher observed that "Jimmy Toner did a really good job with her."[32]

Fleet Indian opened her 2006 season on March 26 by winning the Next Move Handicap (gr.3) on the inner dirt track at Aqueduct. She went off at 4-1 in the four-horse field, the last time she would not be the favorite in a race. Her next start extended her winning streak to four when she took the 9-furlong Sixty Sails Handicap (gr.3) at Hawthorne Park by 12½ lengths. Almost one month later, she won the listed $100,000 Obeah Handicap at Delaware Park by 7¾ lengths as the 3-10 favorite, and on June 16, she won the richest race of her career, the $1 million, 1¼-mile Delaware Handicap (gr.2), by 5½ lengths as the 2-5 favorite. On July 6, she ran her winning streak to seven when she won the 1¼-mile Personal Ensign Handicap (gr.1) at Saratoga by 4½ lengths as the 3-5 favorite. Three months later, she stretched her streak to eight when she won her second straight Grade 1 race, taking the Beldame Stakes by a scant head over Balleto, whom she had easily defeated in the Personal Ensign.

On November 4, Fleet Indian faced the toughest race of her career in the Breeders' Cup Distaff (gr.1) at Churchill Downs. According to the *Blood-Horse*, the field had thirteen Grade 1 winners, and Summerly, the winner of the Kentucky Oaks (gr.1), couldn't even get into the race.[33] Nevertheless, there were only two who went off at short odds, Fleet Indian at 2.70-1 and the 3-year-old Pine Island, 2.90-1, who had previously won the Alabama and Gazelle, both Grade 1s. Tragically, neither crossed the finish line. After getting off to a slow start, Fleet Indian was pulled up at the half-mile pole with what was later diagnosed as a suspensory ligament problem on her left front fetlock joint. She survived, but her racing career was over. Not so fortunate was Pine Island, who fell entering the backstretch and had to be put down. Fleet Indian's 5-year-old season resulted in earnings of $1,473,720, and she was honored with the Eclipse Award for older fillies and mares. She was sold privately to Summer Wind Farm for $3.9 million.

Commentator g. (2001; Distorted Humor— Outsource, by Storm Bird)

Breeder: Michael Martinez
Owner: Tracy Farmer
Trainer: Nick Zito
Jockeys: John Velazquez and Gary Stevens
Career Statistics: 24 starts, 14 wins, 1 second, 4 thirds, $2,049,845

The gelding Commentator raced six years, but because of various physical problems, he only started twenty-four times. This did not stop him from being a favorite of New York bettors, especially at Saratoga. Unraced at two, he had a perfect five-for-five season as a 3-year-old, going gate-to-wire in all his races, winning by a total of 42 lengths. His starts were limited to three New York–bred races, the listed Perryville at Keeneland and an optional claiming allowance at Churchill Downs. None of his races was more than a mile, and he earned $180,692 for his efforts.

He began his 4-year-old season on January 8, finishing seventh in the 9-furlong Hal's Hope Handicap at Gulfstream Park. It was later discovered that he had suffered a shin injury during the race, and he was put on the shelf for six months. After a 16½-length blowout win in an allowance race, he was entered in the 1⅛-mile, $750,000 Whitney Handicap (gr.1) at Saratoga. He and his entrymate, Sir Shackleton, went off at odds of 3-1, while that year's leader in the handicap division, Saint Liam, was the favorite at 7-10. Saint Liam was the highweight in the field at 122 pounds, 6 more than Commentator. As usual, Commentator took the lead and was ahead of Saint Liam by 10 lengths at the three-quarter pole. His rival began closing the gap with every stride, but Commentator's jockey, Gary Stevens, had just enough gas in the tank to beat the favorite by a neck, with Sir Shackleton 9 lengths back in third. A New York–bred speedster who had never won a race beyond a mile and had never won a graded stakes had beaten the best handicap horse in the country. An exultant Nick Zito exclaimed, "This is the most important victory in my life. How can I thank God for this victory?"[34] By that time, Zito had already won two Kentucky Derbies, a Preakness and the first of two Belmont Stakes, and in two weeks he would be inducted into the National Hall of Fame.

Commentator ended his season with a distant third in the Woodward Stake (gr.1), 14½ lengths behind Saint Liam and Sir Shackleton after Saint Liam's trainer Richard Dutrow Jr. had used two rabbits to soften up his front-running rival. In addition, Commentator reinjured his shin during the race and was off for the rest of the year.

The years 2006 and 2007 were not prosperous ones for Commentator. He only raced six times during that period, which probably meant he nursed one or more injuries. He had two wins, none of them in grades stakes, with total earnings of $106,144.

By 2008, he had regained his former winning form. After beginning the year with two romps in an optional claiming race and the Richter Scale Handicap (gr.2) at Gulfstream Park, winning both by a total of 28 lengths, he finished a creditable second as the even-money favorite to Divine Park, the second choice, in the Metropolitan Handicap (gr.1). He then traveled to his favorite track Saratoga, where he thrilled his many fans when he won his second Whitney Stakes (gr.1) by 4½ lengths as the 9-2 second choice. Two months later, he destroyed the field in the $500,000 Massachusetts Handicap, winning by 14 lengths as the 1-10 favorite. He closed out the year by finishing third in the Clark Handicap (gr.2) at Churchill Downs, with Einstein the winner. His 2008 earnings were a lofty $1,068,859.

In 2009, his last year of racing, the 8-year-old finished third in the Charles Town Classic and won the restricted Kashatreya as a tune-up for his final race, a try for a record-setting third win in the Whitney Stakes (gr.1). Almost the betting favorite at 2.20-1 (Smooth Air was the actual favorite at 2.15-1), as well as the sentimental favorite, the best he could do was third, 3 lengths behind Bullsbay and Macho Again. On October 4, he was shipped to Old Friends Thoroughbred Retirement Farm.

BEHAVING BADLY F. (2001; PIONEERING—TIMELEIGHNESS, BY SIR WALTER RALEIGH)

Breeders: Becky Thomas and Lewis Lakin
Owners: Hal Earnhardt and Patti Earnhardt
Trainer: Bob Baffert
Jockey: Victor Espinoza
Career Statistics: 13 starts, 9 wins, 2 seconds, $749,224

The filly sprinter Behaving Badly's home base was California. Unraced at two, she won her only race at three at Del Mar by 8½ lengths and was taken out of training for eight months After beginning her 4-year-old season with an allowance win, she took the Rancho Bernardo Handicap (gr.3) at Del

Mar. Her three-race winning streak was snapped when she came east to run in the Thoroughbred Club of America Stakes (gr.3) at Keeneland. Installed as the even-money favorite, she finished third. She ended the year finishing second in a 6½-furlong sprint on the turf at Santa Anita, her only race in her career on the green, and winning an allowance at Hollywood Park.

She began her 2006 season by taking the Santa Monica Handicap (gr.1) at Santa Anita by 4½ lengths, followed by wins in the Las Flores Handicap (gr.3) and the Bug Brush Stakes. In the latter, she easily defeated the 2005 Test Stakes (gr.1) winner Leave Me Alone. As in 2005, she came east to compete in Kentucky, finishing second, a length behind another Bob Baffert trainee, Pussycat Doll, in the Humana Distaff Handicap (gr.1) on May 4 at Churchill Downs. On July 3, she won the Genuine Risk Breeders' Cup Handicap (gr.2) over three overmatched opponents at Belmont Park, the only time she raced in her native state. She was shipped back to California, and on August 18, she won her second Rancho Bernardo Handicap (gr.3). She returned east, ending her career by losing her second Thoroughbred Club of America Stakes (gr.3) and finishing fourth by 2¼ lengths behind Malibu Mint on the new artificial surface at Keeneland. Her 2006 earnings totaled $552,024.

In addition to her excellent record of nine wins in thirteen starts, three aspects of her career stand out: only thirteen starts in three years, a reflection of the many injuries and ailments Baffert had to contend with; her record of one win (against only three opponents) in four starts on the East Coast, compared with eight wins in nine starts (her only loss was her only race on the turf) in California; and the fact that in her thirteen starts, she was the favorite in twelve of them, the only exception when she was the 3-2 second choice.

FRIENDLY ISLAND c. (2001; CRAFTY FRIEND—ISLAND QUEEN, BY OGYGIAN)

Breeder: Kildare Stud (Frankie and Anne O'Connors)
Owner: Antsu Stable (Stuart and Adrian Regan)
Trainers: Todd Pletcher and Michael McCarthy
Jockey: John Velazquez
Career Statistics: 19 starts, 8 wins, 3 seconds, 2 thirds, $1,369,714

The sprinter Friendly Island earned almost $1.4 million while winning only two Grade 3 events. Unraced at two, in 2004 he won five of seven starts, four in state-bred events. In his graded stakes debut, he finished seventh in the Fall Highweight Handicap (gr.3). He had only two starts in 2005, with his second win in the Hudson Handicap for New York–breds and a fourth in the DeFrancis Memorial Dash (gr.1) at Laurel Park. His combined earnings for his first two years came to $265,218—not chump change, but nothing exceptional.

It was in 2006 that Friendly Island became noticed by the general racing public. He raced eight times, all graded events, beginning on January 7 with a third as the 2-1 favorite in the Mr. Prospector Handicap (gr.3) at Gulfstream Park. After a sixth in the Deputy Minister (gr.3), he traveled to Arkansas, where he finished second in the Count Fleet Sprint Handicap (gr.3) at 9-1, 1½ lengths behind Boronaro. Five weeks later, on May 20, he won the Maryland Breeders' Cup Handicap (gr.3) as the 3-2 favorite. After a seventh in the Smile Sprint Handicap (gr.2) at Calder, he finished third in the Forego Handicap (gr.1) at Saratoga at odds of 36-1, 2½ lengths behind Pomeroy (6-1) and War Front (5-1), with Commentator finishing eleventh as the 9-10 favorite. In the next to last race of the season, he checked in seventh in the one-mile Kelso Handicap (gr.2T) at Belmont Park, the only time he raced on the turf, although judging by his next race Pletcher might have been using the turf-to-dirt angle. Friendly Island ended his 2006 season with the best performance of his career thus far, finishing second in the Breeders' Cup Sprint at odds of 58-1, 4 lengths behind Thor's Echo (15-1). Among the also-rans were old foes Nightmare Affair, Boronaro, War Front and Pomeroy. The $426,000 he collected from that race was by far the biggest payoff of his career and boosted his 2006 earnings to $614,500.

Friendly Island only had two starts in his last year of racing in 2007, opening the season in California with a win in the Palos Verdes Handicap (gr.3) at Santa Anita as the 1-2 favorite. It was the first stakes win for Michael McCarthy, who was handling Pletcher's horses in California while Pletcher was serving a forty-five-day suspension. On March 31, in the last race of his career, Friendly Island had another lucrative payday when he finished second to Kelly's Landing in the $2 million Dubai Golden Shaheen (gr.1). His two starts in 2007 resulted in earnings of $490,000. He was retired to stud duty at Howard and Susan Kaskel's Sugar Maple Farm near Poughquag, New York, where he was born.

Read the Footnotes c. (2001; Smoke Glacken— Baydon Belle, by Al Nasr)

Breeder: Lawrence Goichman
Owner: Klaravich Stables (Seth Klarman)
Trainer: Rick Violette
Jockey: Jerry Bailey
Career Statistics: 8 starts, 5 wins, $450,660

Although he had a short career, at one time Read the Footnotes was considered one of the favorites for the Kentucky Derby. He began to show promise as a 2-year-old, winning his debut on August 17 in a 2-year-old maiden special weight race for New York–breds by 9¼ lengths at Saratoga. Three weeks later, he won an allowance against open company at Belmont by 2½ lengths as the 1-2 favorite. His road to Louisville took a detour when he finished sixth in the Champagne Stake (gr.1), 15 lengths behind the winner, Birdstone, who would later win the 2004 Belmont (gr.1) and Travers (gr.1). He finished the year by winning the Nashua (gr.3) and Remsen (gr.2). His earnings for his 2-year-old season were $240,660.

Read the Footnotes continued his success by opening his 3-year-old season winning his third graded stake in a row, taking the 1¹/₁₆-mile Fountain of Youth Stakes (gr.2) at Gulfstream Park by a neck over Second of June. Bill Finley declared, "Not only is [Rick Violette's] horse good, he's tough. That is the sort of combination that can make a horse a winner in the Kentucky Derby."[35] It was also mentioned by more than one turf writer that the previous winner of the Kentucky Derby was another New York–bred named Funny Cide.

The next stop on the way to Louisville was the Florida Derby (gr.1). The bettors made Read the Footnotes the favorite, with Value Plus and Cliff's Edge the second and third choices. The race was, in fact, won by a New York–bred, but it was not Read the Footnotes, who finished fifth, 5 lengths behind the winner, Chester and Mary Broman's 37-1 shot Friends Lake. Violette decided to train his colt up to the Kentucky Derby, but the result was no better, as Read the Footnotes finished fifth at 22-1, 15 lengths behind the winner, the 4-1 favorite Smarty Jones. He came out of the race with a chipped knee, which required surgery. Although an article in the *Daily Racing Form* stated that he would make his comeback on December 26 in the Malibu (gr.1) at Santa Anita,[36] he never raced again, and he was retired to stud at Sequel Farms in Florida.

Capeside Lady f. (2001; Cape Town—Gray Lady Type, by Zen)

Breeders: Becky Thomas, Brenda Lakin and Lewis Lakin
Owners: So Madcapt Stable; Dapple Stable
Trainers: Todd Pletcher; Scott Blasi
Jockeys: Chris DeCarlo and John Velazquez
Career Statistics: 21 starts, 8 wins, 3 seconds, 3 thirds, $809,540

Capeside Lady was a front-running, mud-loving filly who had most of her top moments at Monmouth Park. In her 2-year-old season, she broke her maiden at first asking by 8½ lengths at Belmont Park, finished eighth in the Sorority (gr.3) at Monmouth Park and won the restricted Joseph H. Gimma and Maid o' The Mist at Belmont, giving her earnings of $149,940.

After beginning her 2004 season with thirds in the restricted Bouwerie and open Funistrada Stakes, she returned to what was to be her favorite track, Monmouth Park. She won the Little Silver Stakes by 13½ lengths on a sloppy track, followed on August 1 by a win in the Monmouth Breeders' Cup Oaks by 6½ lengths as the 3-2 favorite on a muddy oval, setting a track record of 1:42 for the 8½-furlong distance. She ended her season with a second in the Indiana Oaks and fourths in the Turnback the Alarm Handicap (gr.3) at Aqueduct and the Francis A. Genter at Calder, giving her earnings for the year of $266,220.

She began her 2005 season on May 30 by finishing a disappointing seventh in the Fort Monmouth. On June 18, she won the Monmouth Beach by 5½ lengths as the even-money favorite, followed on July 9 by a five-length score in the Molly Pitcher Handicap (gr.2) on a muddy Monmouth Park track as the 3-2 favorite. She ended her season with a sixth in the Ruffian Handicap (gr.1) at Belmont, a third in the Spinster (gr.1) at Keeneland and a sixth in the Breeders' Cup Distaff (gr.1) at Belmont Park, with earnings of $278,600.

In 2016, she had a change in connections, with a new owner, Dapple Stable, and a new trainer, Scott Blasi. She raced four times, with a win in the Bayakoa at Oaklawn Park as the 7-10 favorite, a fifth in the Louisville Handicap (gr.2) at Churchill Downs and seconds in the Iowa Distaff at Prairie Downs and the Lady's Secret at Monmouth Park as the even-money favorite. She earned $114,780 in 2016.

J'ray f. (2003; Distant View—Bubbling Heights, by Darshaan)

Breeder/Owner: Lawrence Goichman
Trainers: Todd Pletcher and Anthony Sciametta Jr.
Jockey: no main jockey
Career Statistics: 26 starts, 9 wins, 8 seconds, 1 third, $969,843

Even as a 2-year-old, J' ray was considered one of the leading distaff turf runners of her generation, but she didn't win her first graded stakes until February of her 4-year-old season. After finishing sixth in her debut, a 2-year-old state-bred maiden special weight race on Belmont Park's dirt track, her dominating win in a maiden turf event at Saratoga guaranteed that her future belonged on the grass. Her next start, the $100,000 Jessamine County Stakes at Keeneland, resulted in her first stakes win, and it was followed on November 18 with a win in the $125,000 Selima Stakes at Laurel Park by 3¾ lengths as the 2-1 favorite. On January 1, she celebrated New Year's Day by stretching her winning streak to four in the Tropical Park Oaks at Calder as the prohibitive 1-2 favorite.

She didn't start again until April 22, when she finished third as the 6-5 favorite in Appalachian Stakes at Keeneland. After a four-month layoff, she returned in the Valley View (gr.3T) at Keeneland, where she finished sixth after it was switched to the main track. It would be her last start on the dirt. On November 15, she lost the Revere Stakes (gr.2T) by a head at Churchill Downs, beginning a frustrating three-race streak in which she would lose graded stakes by narrow margins. On December 29, she lost the Francis A. Genter (gr.3T) at Calder to Bayou's Lassie. For this race and the one after that, she was trained by assistant trainer Anthony Sciametta Jr. after Todd Pletcher was given a lengthy suspension. She earned $122,973 in 2006.

On February 3, 2007, J'ray lost by a neck to Naissance Royale in the Suwanne River Handicap (gr.3T) at Gulfstream Park at 7-2. In her last three races, all graded stakes, she lost by a neck, a head and a neck. On February 24, she celebrated Todd Pletcher's return by winning her first graded stakes, taking the Bayou Breeders' Cup Handicap (gr.3T) at Fair Grounds by 4¾ lengths as the 1-10 favorite. One month later, she made it two in a row when she took the listed Marie G. Krantz Memorial Handicap by 3½ lengths as the 2-5 favorite at Fair Grounds. She then went on a three-race losing streak, finishing second in the Dr. J. Penny at

Philadelphia and off the board in the Yaddo and Ticonderoga Stakes for New York–breds, earning $227,471 for the year.

Although 2008 was the most lucrative of her career, J' ray began the season with five straight losses, eight in all, beginning on February 3 by finishing third, half a length behind the winner Green Girl, as the 2-1 favorite in the Suwanee River Handicap (gr.3T). She was subsequently moved up to second after Green Girl was disqualified. On March 8, she finished fourth, half a length behind the winner, Mauralakana in The Very One (gr.3T) at Gulfstream Park, once again as the 2-1 favorite. She also lost her next two races to that foe in the $300,000 Mairzy Doates at Calder and the Sheepshead Bay Handicap (gr.2T) at Belmont Park. On June 28, she capped her losing streak when she finished fifth at 3-1 in the All Along Breeders' Cup (gr.3T) at Colonial Downs.

On August 8, she won her first race of the year when she took the Matchmaker (gr.3T) at 5-1 at Monmouth Park. On September 7, she won the Canadian (gr.2T) on a yielding Woodbine turf course at 6-1. Finishing third was Forever Together, who had previously won the Diana Handicap (gr.1T) at Saratoga. J' ray closed out her season and her career by finishing fourth in the E.P. Taylor (gr.1T) at Woodbine and second in the Long Island Handicap (gr.2T) at Aqueduct and the 1½-mile La Prevoyante (gr.2T) at Calder, losing by a neck to Herboriste while conceding five pounds to that opponent. She made $462,154 in 2008.

SILVER TIMBER G. (2003; PRIME TIMBER—RIVER PRINCESS, BY ALWUHUSH)

Breeder: Sez Who Thoroughbreds
Owners: Invictus Farm; Michael Dubb
Trainers: Linda Rice; Chad Brown
Jockeys: Julien Leparoux and Eibar Coa
Career Statistics: 49 starts, 14 wins, 6 seconds, 9 thirds, $774,680

The turf sprinter Silver Timber was originally owned by Invictus Farm and trained by Linda Rice from 2005 through 2008. He was relatively unknown, with no stakes wins of any kind to his credit. On April 12, 2009, in his first start of the season, he was claimed for $25,000 by trainer Chad Brown for Michael Dubb, and he was a new horse from that point on.

Silver Timber won the first race he ran under Brown's tutelage, an optional claimer on May 15 at Belmont Park. His next start two months later was his successful debut in graded stakes, taking the 6-furlong Jaipur (gr.3T) by 1½ lengths at odds of 7-2, which gave him a winning streak of three (he also won the race in which he was claimed). On September 6, that streak was broken when he lost the 5½-furlong Commentator Stakes for New York–breds by a neck on the turf at Saratoga. He then traveled to Kentucky, where he won the 5½-furlong Woodford (gr.3T) on a soft Keeneland turf course. He ended his 6-year-old season in California, finishing sixth in the Breeders' Cup Turf Sprint (gr.2T), 4½ lengths from the winner, California Flag. The New York–bred Cannonball, who had beaten him in the Commentator, finished third. Silver Timber ended his season with earnings of $193,740, approximately $20,000 less than he made in his first four years of racing.

He began his 2010 campaign on April 10 by winning the Shakertown (gr.3T) at Keeneland as the 3-2 favorite, with the 1.80-1 second choice Chamberlain Bridge fourth. Two weeks later, he won the Churchill Downs Turf Sprint (gr.3T) by a neck over Chamberlain Bridge, despite conceding six pounds to that rival. In the process, he set a new track record of 0:55.45 for the 5-furlong distance. He then traveled north, winning the Wolf Hill and finishing second in the John McSorly at Monmouth Park and fifth in the Troy Handicap at Saratoga as the 3-5 favorite. He returned to his home base at Keeneland, where the *Blood-Horse* claimed that he liked training on that track's artificial dirt surface.[37] That must have been the cure, because he on October 9 he won his second Woodford (gr.3T) at Keeneland. He went off at odds of 4-1 in a strong field that included the 3-2 favorite California Flag, winner of the 2009 Breeders' Cup Turf Sprint, who finished last, and the 3-1 second choice, Chamberlain Bridge, winner of his last three races, who finished fourth. The bettors obviously overlooked the Keeneland training angle.

The Woodford would be the last stakes win of his career. He ended the year finishing fifth in the Breeders' Cup Turf Sprint (gr.2T) at Churchill Downs, at least partly due to a troubled trip. Finishing first was his old rival Chamberlain Bridge, 6-1, and finishing second was Central City, 9-1, who had finished third to Silver Timber in the Churchill Downs Turf Sprint and second to him in the Woodford. The chart summary read, "Silver Timber bobbled at the break, was sent up three wide between horses nearing the turn…briefly lost his momentum when Chamberlain Bridge bore out near the sixteenth marker then finished up well in the final yards."[38] He ended the year with earnings of $296,511. In 2011 and 2012, he clearly felt his age, winning only one race in twelve starts, and was retired.

OPRAH WINNEY F. (2003; ROYAL ACADEMY—MERE PRESENCE, BY WOODMAN)

Breeder: Gatsas Thoroughbreds Ltd.
Owners: Sanford Goldfarb, Michael Dubb and Bunch of Characters Stable
Trainers: Richard Dutrow Jr. and Anthony Dutrow
Jockey: no main jockey
Career Statistics: 18 starts, 7 wins, 3 seconds, 5 thirds, $593,989

The filly sprinter Oprah Winney had two successful seasons as a 2- and 3-year-old but did not become a star until she was 4. She won more than $180,000 from eight starts in 2005 and 2006, her only stakes win being in the Bouwerie for New York–breds.

She began her breakout year on January 1, 2007, by taking the listed Interborough Handicap at Aqueduct at odds of 11-1. It would be the last time she would go off at double-digit odds. Her next race, on February 17, was the highlight of her career, winning the 7-furlong Barbara Fritchie Handicap (gr.2) at Laurel, going gate-to-wire at odds of 3.20-1. Finishing second was the 3.10 second favorite Silmaril, with the 2-1 favorite Leah's Secret in fifth. For this race only, she was trained by Tony Dutrow, who was subbing for his brother Richard Dutrow Jr., who was serving a fourteen-day suspension.

She lost her next two races, finishing third in the Distaff Breeders' Cup Handicap (gr.2) at Aqueduct and second in the Vagrancy Handicap (gr.2) at odds of 2.95-1, half a length behind the winner Indian Flare, the 2.65-1 favorite. On August 5, she won the $100,000 Regret at Monmouth as the 3-5 favorite, and one month later, she took the restricted $104,000 Schenectady Handicap as the 1-10 favorite. The last two races of her career were disappointments, finishing eighth in the Breeders' Cup Filly and Mare Sprint at Monmouth at 6-1 and third in the Garland of Roses at Aqueduct as the 4-5 favorite. In March 2008, she was retired to be a broodmare at Hidden Brook near Paris, Kentucky.

GET SERIOUS G. (2004; CITY ZIP—JAVA GIRL, BY JAVA GOLD)

Breeder: Morgan's Ford Farm (Suzie and Wayne Chatfield-Taylor)
Owners: James Dinan, Jacques J. Moore, Phantom House Farm
Trainers: John H. Forbes; Patrick McBurney
Jockey: Pablo Fragoso
Career Statistics: 43 starts, 14 wins, 2 seconds, 5 thirds, $1,124,651

A May foal, Get Serious was unraced as a 2-year-old. After moderate success at Monmouth Park in his first four starts, he finished eleventh in the Pennsylvania Derby (gr.1), followed by three off-the-board performances in his home state, ending 2011 and beginning 2012 with two similar results in Philadelphia. Three of his first ten races were on the turf, including an allowance win at Monmouth. After a third and a sixth at Philadelphia and a fourth and a win in turf allowances at Monmouth and a seventh in the Monmouth Stakes, on October 18 he returned to New York, losing the Alex M. Robb by a neck on the turf at Belmont. On November 14, he won his first stake, taking the listed Alysheba on a sloppy Meadowlands main track, and he ended his 4-year-old season by traveling back to New York for the last time, finishing eighth in the Alex M. Robb Handicap for New York–breds on Aqueduct's inner dirt track.

In 2009, he experienced a renaissance, becoming one of the better turf horses at Monmouth. He began by winning two listed turf races, the Elkwood and Battlefield, sandwiched between a fifth in the Skip Away on Monmouth's dirt track, followed by a win in the Oceanport, which was ungraded after being taken off the turf. On September 6, he won his first graded stakes, taking the first of his three wins in the Red Bank (gr.3T), setting a new track record of 1:32 for the mile distance. He ended the year on October 3 with a fifth in the Cliff Hanger (gr.3T) on a yielding Meadowlands course. All the rest of his New Jersey races were at Monmouth. His earnings for 2009 were $314,810.

He began his 2010 season with a turf allowance win, followed by a win in the Monmouth Stakes (gr.3T) and a fifth in the United Nations Handicap (gr.1T). He ended his short season with wins in the Oceanport (gr.3T) and Red Bank (gr.3T), giving him earnings of $459,500.

He began a downward slide in 2011, with off-the-board performances in the Elkwood, Monmouth (gr.3T), Battlefield and Cliff Hanger (gr.3T), continuing into 2012 with a sixth in the Elkwood and a third in the

Monmouth (gr.2T). His next race on July 4, his third win in the Red Bank (gr.3T), was the last win of his career. After thirds in the Oceanport (gr.3T) and Cliff Hanger (gr.3T), he took a three-month break to recover from an injury, and on December 12, he began in a new track, Gulfstream Park, with a new trainer, Patrick McBurney. He finished off the board in three races in Florida in 2012 and two races in 2013 before being retired.

Mission Approved c. (2004; With Approval— Fortunate Find, by Fortunate Prospect)

Breeder: Dr. William E. Coyro Jr.
Owners: Dr. William E. Coyro Jr.; Naipaul Chatterpaul and Terikchaud
* Chatterpaul*
Trainers: Gary Contessa; Naipaul Chatterpaul
Jockey: no main jockey
Career Statistics: 29 starts 8 wins, 5 seconds, 1 third, $827,210

Mission Approved was a front-running turf specialist who had success with one trainer/owner, was claimed and had success with another owner. Unraced at two, after winning two of his first four starts in 2007 against New York–breds, he switched to the turf and never raced on dirt the rest of his career. After two off-the-board finishes in the listed Lexington and Glow Stakes on the turf, on September 2 he won his first graded stakes, the $1^3/_{16}$-mile Saranac (gr.3T) at Saratoga at odds of 34-1, followed by another win in the Princeton at the Meadowlands. He ended his season on September 30 by finishing fifth in the Turf Classic Invitational Handicap (gr.1T) at odds of 16-1. His 2007 earnings were $219,332 from ten starts.

With one exception, 2008 was a lost year for Mission Approved. He started four times, finishing seventh in three of them, two New York–bred stakes and the Man o' War (gr.1T). The only exception was a win in the Singspiel Stakes (gr.3T) at Woodbine, giving him earnings of $90,683 for the year. Things improved slightly in 2009, finishing second twice and fourth twice in his first four races, but his season ended on August 16 when he ran eighth in the West Point Handicap for New York–breds. His earnings were a paltry, for him, $56,415.

He began 2010 being claimed for $35,000 by Naipaul Chatterpaul on May 11 in a winning effort in a claiming race at Delaware Park. One month later, he finished second in an optional claiming race for his new connections, and on July 10, he lost the Man o' War Stakes (gr.1T) by a neck to the 2009 and 2010 male turf champion Gio Ponti at odds of 53-1. That race was the last one for the year, giving him earnings of $150,400, more than compensating his new owners for his $35,000 price tag.

Mission Approved continued his renaissance when he opened his 2011 season on June 11 by winning the 1¼-mile Manhattan Handicap (gr.1T) at odds of 21-1, with the 3-2 favorite Gio Ponti 1½ lengths behind in third, conceding seven pounds to the winner.

The Manhattan would be Mission Approval's last hurrah, as he ended the season and his career with losses in the Man o' War (gr.1T), fourth; the Arlington Million (gr.1T), seventh; the Turf Classic Invitational (gr.1T), fourth; and the Japan Cup in Tokyo (gr.1T), fourteenth. He was retired after the Japan Cup, with his stud plans pending his sale at auction.

PAYS TO DREAM G. (2004; HIGH YIELD—CHANGING WAYS, BY TIME FOR A CHANGE)

Owner and Breeder: December Hill Farm (Dragone family)
Trainer: David Donk
Jockey: Javier Castellano
Career Statistics: 15 starts, 5 wins, 1 second, 4 thirds, $377,741

Unraced at two, Pays to Dream began his career on January 6, 2007, losing his first three races until he made a successful switch to the turf. After two more wins against New York–breds and a third against open company, he raced in the listed Lexington, finishing fourth. On August 4 at Saratoga, he won his first stake, the Glow, at 9-1. On September 2, he finished third in the Saranac Stakes (gr.3T) at Saratoga, 1½ lengths behind the winner, Mission Approved. Five weeks later, he finished third in the Jamaica Handicap (gr.2T), and he ended his season in the Rutgers at the Meadowlands when he stumbled coming out of the gate, throwing his jockey. His earnings for the year were $186,635.

He began his 4-year-old season by finishing seventh in the Fort Marcy Handicap (gr.3T). On May 1, he won the biggest race of his career, taking the Dixie Stakes (gr.2T) by 7½ lengths on a good Pimlico turf course at odds of 19-1. The ability he showed in the Dixie was also evident in the

Manhattan Handicap (gr.1T), when he finished third at odds of 11-1, half a length behind the winner, Dancing Forever. Unfortunately, he was vanned off and never ran again, putting an unfortunate end to what looked like a promising career.

Bustin Stones c. (2004; City Zip—Shesasurething, by Prospectors Gamble)

Breeder/Owner: Roddy Valente
Trainer: Bruce Levine
Jockey: Ramon Dominguez
Career Statistics: 6 starts, 6 wins, $480,150

The sprinter Bustin Stones won all six of his races in gate-to-wire fashion. A May foal, he did not begin racing until his 3-year-old season. He began his career on March 24, 2007, by winning a New York–bred maiden special weight race and ended his brief season by taking the restricted New York Stallion Times Square at Aqueduct and the Screenland at Belmont, earning $124,650 from his three races. His time off was necessitated by lingering foot problems.

He made his 2008 debut on January 21 by taking the Promonroe at Aqueduct and, five weeks later, won his first graded stakes, the $300,000 General George Handicap (gr.2) at Laurel as the 2-1 favorite. After the race, jockey Ramon Dominguez described what it's like to ride Bustin Stones: "He is a dream horse to ride because he is like a Quarter Horse coming out of the gate. By the second jump, he is listening to you. He would go 21 with no problem, but as soon as you put your hands down, he relaxes."[39]

On April 5, in what was to be the last race of his career, he took the 7-furlong Carter Handicap (gr.1) at Aqueduct as the 5-2 second choice. The even-money favorite, Spring at Last, who had previously won the Donn Handicap (gr.1) at Gulfstream Park, finished eighth. After the Carter, Bustin Stones was given time to deal with recurring foot problems. He was scheduled to start in the Alfred G. Vanderbilt (gr.2) at Saratoga as the 2-1 morning line favorite, with his eventual goal the Breeders' Cup Sprint, but his foot problems forced his retirement. In 2009, he began stud duty at Dr. Jerry Belinsky's Waldorf Farm.

A SHIN FORWARD C. (2005; FOREST WILDCAT—WAKE UP KISS, BY CURE THE BLUES)

Breeder: Edition Farm (Vivien Malloy)
Owner: Eshindo Company Ltd.
Trainer: Masato Nishizono
Jockey: Yasunani Iwata
Career Statistics: 31 starts, 6 wins, 3 seconds, 3 thirds, $3,421,360

A Shin Forward was a turf sprinter who spent his entire career in Japan. In his first three years of racing, he finished second in the 2008 Arlington Cup at Hanshin and the New Zealand Trophy at Nakayana and won the 2009 Rokko Island and Final Stakes at Hanshin. He began the 2010 season by winning the New Year Stakes at Nakayama, followed by a third in the Tokyo Shimbun Hai (gr.3T). On February 28, he won his first graded stakes, taking the Hankyu Hai (gr.3T), and one month later finished third in the Takamatsunomiya Kinen (gr.1) at Chukyo. On November 21, he had his greatest victory, taking the Mile Championship (gr.1T) at Kyoto at odds of 52-1. After six losing efforts in 2011, he retired to take up stud duty at Lex Stud in Hokkaido, and in February 2012, he returned to the place of his birth to stand for Edition Farm. When he retired, he was the second-richest New York–bred in history after Funny Cide.

Opposite: A Shin Forward winning the Hankyu Hai at Hanshin. *Japan Racing Association.*

Above: A Shin Forward in the winners' circle after winning the Hankyu Hai. *Japan Racing Association.*

HAYNESFIELD C. (2006; SPEIGHTSTOWN—NOTHING SPECIAL, BY TEJABO)

Breeders: Barry Weisbrod and Margaret Santulli
Owners: Vision Racing; Turtle Bird Stable (Harvey Weinstein)
Trainer: Steve Asmussen
Jockey: Ramon Dominguez
Career Statistics: 19 starts, 10 wins, 2 seconds, 1 third, $1,319,481

Haynesfield was bought by Harvey Weinstein's Turtle Stable after his second start. Although Steve Asmussen was the nominal trainer for both Vision Racing and Weinstein, the day-by-day care and decisions for Haynesfield were made by Asmussen's assistant, Toby Sheets, who had persuaded Weinstein to buy the horse.

After breaking his maiden on September 25 of his 2-year-old season, he ended the year by taking the restricted Damon Runyon, and he began 2009 by winning the listed Count Fleet and Whirlaway Stakes on the inner dirt track at Aqueduct. That modest four-race winning streak encouraged his connections to think about the Kentucky Derby. Those dreams were abandoned after he finished eighth in the Gotham (gr.3), 26 lengths behind the winner, I Want Revenge, and was given seven months off. On October 2, he finished second in the Sir Key, followed by a win in the Empire Classic, both restricted to New York–breds. He ended the season by taking the 1⅛-mile Discovery Handicap (gr.3) by 4½ lengths as the 7-2 third choice in the six horse field. His earnings in 2009 were a healthy $334,216.

It was as a 4-year-old that Haynesfield became a star, taking on the best handicap horses in the East. He opened the year on June 13 by winning an optional claiming race for New York–breds and followed that by taking the Suburban Handicap (gr.2) at Belmont Park at odds of 7-2. Finishing third was the even-money favorite, I Want Revenge, who hadn't raced since winning the 2009 Wood Memorial (gr.1). On August 2, Haynesfield made his Grade 1 debut in the Whitney at Saratoga finishing fourth at odds of 12-1. Finishing ahead of him were the winner, Blame, who would eventually be named that year's champion older male after winning the Breeders' Cup Classic; the 1-2 favorite Quality Road, winner of the Donn (gr.1) and Metropolitan (gr.1) Handicaps; and Musket Man.

Haynesfield, Ramon Dominguez up, warming up prior to the 2010 Whitney. *Michele Williams.*

On October 2, he hit the big time when he won the won the Jockey Club Gold Cup (gr.1), going gate to wire at odds of 7-1. Finishing second, $4\frac{1}{2}$ lengths behind, was the 4-5 favorite Blame. It was Haynesfield's fifth win in six starts at Belmont Park, and the $450,000 he made in that race put him over the $1 million mark for lifetime earnings. He finished eleventh to Blame and Zenyatta in the Breeders' Cup Classic (gr.1) and ended the year three weeks later by finishing second in the Cigar Mile (gr.1), a head behind the 71-1 long shot Jersey Town. His 2010 earnings were $749,300.

After opening the 2011 season with a fourth in the Westchester Handicap (gr.3) and a fifth in the Metropolitan Handicap (gr.1), he took some time off to heal a sore foot, He returned on October 2 to win his second Empire Classic and ended his career with a fourth in the Cigar Mile (gr.1). In 2012, he began stud duty with Airdrie Stud in Midway, Kentucky.

Rightly So f. (2006; Read the Footnotes—Fit Right In, by Out of Place)

Breeder: Sequel 2003 Stable (Becky Thomas and Lewis Lakin)
Owner: Ahmed Zayat
Trainer: Tony Dutrow
Jockeys: Ramon Dominguez and Cornelio Velasquez
Career Statistics: 11 starts, 7 wins, 2 seconds, 1 third, $480,050

Unraced at two, Rightly So began her career on January 3, 2009, by finishing second in a maiden race for New York–breds. She then ended her 3-year-old season with five straight wins, including the Iroquois for New York–breds and the listed Love is Eternal. Her earnings for 2009 were $201,550.

She started her 4-year-old season by finishing third as the 3-5 favorite in the restricted Broadway Stakes, a neck behind the winner, Lights Off Annie. This race was notable because it was the only race in her career when she finished worse than second. In her next race, she finished second by a nose in the Distinctly, also for New York–breds. On May 29, she placed second in the $6\frac{1}{2}$-furlong Vagrancy Handicap (gr.2) at Belmont Park, half a length behind Hour Glass at odds of 12-1. She lost her first three races as a 4-year-old by a total of $1\frac{1}{4}$ lengths and would not lose another race. On July 5, she won her first graded race, taking the 7-furlong

Rightly So, Cornelio Velasquez in the irons, while winning the 2010 Ballerina. *Michele Williams.*

Bed O'Roses Handicap (gr.3) at odds of 7-2, beating the even-money favorite Qualia by a head. On August 29, she won what was to be the last race of her career when she won the Ballerina Stakes (gr.1) at Saratoga by an emphatic 4 lengths, going gate to wire as the 9-2 third favorite. Finishing sixth was the favorite, Informed Decision, winner of the 2009 Breeders' Cup Filly and Mare Sprint. Her next scheduled start was the Breeders' Cup Breeders' Cup Filly and Mare Sprint (gr.1) on November 5 at Churchill Downs. Despite drawing the thirteen post, she was installed as the 3-1 morning line favorite, with Informed Decision the second favorite at 7-2. However, on the morning of the race, the Breeders' Cup Veterinary Panel didn't like the way she moved, and she was scratched. It was later determined that she was lame, and she was retired. Her 2010 earnings were $278,500 from only five starts. She was sold for $600,000 to Patinack Farm in Australia.

GIANT RYAN C. (2006; FREUD—KHEYRAH, BY DAYJUR)

Breeder: Sequel Stables (Becky Thomas and Lewis Lakin)
Owner: Shivananda Parbhoo
Trainer: Bisnath Parbhoo
Jockey: Cornelio Velasquez
Career Statistics: 17 starts, 8 wins, 1 second, 1 third, $686,841

The sprinter Giant Ryan did not reach his peak until his 5-year-old season. Whether because of injury or design, he only raced six times from 2008 through 2010, with two wins and one second, earning $67,351. His only stakes experiences were a fifth in the restricted Jimmy Winkfield and a ninth in the Gotham (gr.3). It was in 2011 that Giant Ryan faced and defeated some of the best sprinters in the east. That season started slowly, losing two races at Gulfstream Park before coming north and winning three straight races, including the restricted Hamlet Stakes. He then made a return trip to Florida, where on June 11 he won the listed Ponche Handicap at Calder Race Course as the 3-5 favorite. One month later, he won his first graded stake, taking Calder's Smile Sprint Handicap (gr.2) at odds of 7-1, a neck in front of Irrefutable, with the 3-2 favorite Noble's Promise third. Giant Ryan's two races at Calder were so impressive that track executives named a race after him in 2012.

Giant Ryan returned to New York, and on October 1, he won the Vosburgh Invitational (gr.1) on a muddy Belmont Park track by half a length at odds of 12-1. Finishing fourth was the even-money favorite, Trappe Shot, who had previously won the True North Handicap (gr.2) by 8½ lengths, and finishing eighth and last was Bob Baffert's Euroears, the 2-1 second choice, who had previously won the Bing Crosby (gr.1) at Del Mar. The Vosburgh was Giant Ryan's sixth straight win and the last of his career. He ended the season by finishing eighth in the Breeders' Cup Sprint at Churchill Downs. He nevertheless had a stellar 2011 record of six wins from nine starts, with earnings of $559,490.

Giant Ryan's 2012 season illustrated the highs and lows that occasionally happen in the sport. He began the year on March 31 by finishing fifth in the $2 million Dubai Golden Shaheen (gr.1) after leading for most of the race. In his next start, the True North Handicap (gr.2) on June 9 at Belmont Park, he was battling Caixa Electronica for the lead when he fractured both left sesamoids. On June 14, he was euthanized due to complications from his injuries.

FRANNY FREUD F. (2007; FREUD—FRANKLY FRAN, BY D'ACCORD)

Breeder: Anthony Grey
Owners: Paul Pompa Jr., Stephen Yarborough and Winter Park Partners
Trainer: John Terranova II
Jockey: Garrett Gomez
Career Statistics: 11 starts, 8 wins, 2 seconds, $686,029

The sprinter Franny Freud had a very promising beginning, winning her first race of her 2-year-old season in a maiden event against males on May 29 by 7 lengths. She also won the Ontario Debutante at Woodbine, the Lady Finger at Finger Lakes and the New York Stallion Fifth Avenue at Belmont Park and was second in the My Dear Stakes at Woodbine. Her only off-the-board performance was in the Frizette (gr.1), finishing fifth to Devil May Care, who as a 3-year-old would win the Mother Goose (gr.1). She ended her season with earnings of $269,069.

She began her 3-year-old season on January 12 in California, finishing second in the Santa Ynez, ¾ of a length behind Amen Hallelujah. She was the second choice at 2-1, the only time that year that she was not the favorite and the only time she ran at odds of more than 7-10. It would also be the only time she lost that season. After returning to the East Coast, she won the Beaumont Stakes (gr.2) on April 17 on Keeneland's artificial dirt track at odds of 1-2. On May 2, she took the New York Stallion Park Avenue by 7¾ lengths at odds of 1-4. On May 26, she showed her versatility when she beat the boys on the turf in the 7-furlong New York Stallion by 6 lengths at odds of 1-4. She won her last race of the year on July 4 when she took the Prioress Stakes (gr.1) at Belmont by 1¾ lengths at odds of 7-10. The filly who finished second, Champagne d'Oro, had earlier won the Acorn (gr.1).

After the Prioress, she was scheduled to start in the Test Stakes (gr.1) at Saratoga and was made the morning line favorite at 5-2. However, three days before the race, it was announced that she had sustained a ligament injury in a workout and was forced to retire. Her 2010 earnings were $390,000. Later that year, she was sold for $560,000 to Katsumi Yoshida in Hokkaido, Japan.

Dayatthespa f. (2009; City Zip—M'Lady Doc, by Doc's Leader)

Breeder: Castellare DiCracciolo Stable, Scott Goldsher
Owners: Jerry Frankel and Robert Frankel, Steve Laymon (Peter Bradley, Charles Bales, Tom Jackson, Kris Kruid and Clay Sanders)
Trainer: Chad Brown
Jockey: Javier Castellano
Career Statistics: 18 starts, 11 wins, 4 seconds, $2,288,892

In 2012 and 2014, Dayatthespa was one of best filly and mare turf horses in the country. In her three starts as a 2-year-old, she broke her maiden at first asking at Saratoga, lost the Natalma (gr.2T) at Woodbine by 1½ lengths and finished ninth to Stephanie's Kitten in the Breeders' Cup Juvenile Turf (gr.2T) on a soft Churchill Downs turf.

In 2012, she raced six times, won five of those six starts and was the favorite in five of them. She began on January 22 with a win in the $100,000 Sweetest Chant at Gulfstream Park as the even-money favorite. On March 11, she won her first graded stakes, taking the 1⅛-mile Herecomesthebride (gr.3T) at Gulfstream as the 9-10 favorite. Five weeks later, she won her third stakes in a row, taking the Appalachian (gr.3T) at Keeneland as the 6-5 favorite. After a break of four and a half months, she won the listed Riskaverse at Saratoga at odds of 1-2. On October 13, she faced the toughest field of her career thus far in the 1⅛-mile Queen Elizabeth II Challenge Cup (gr.1T) at Keeneland as the second choice at odds of 3-1. Despite not being the favorite, she shook off the slight, winning by 2 lengths going gate to wire. Finishing sixth was the 2-1 favorite Stephanie's Kitten. Finishing fourth at 7-2 was the 2012 Irish 1000 Guineas (gr.1T) winner, Samitar. Dayatthespa ended her season and her five-race winning streak by finishing fifth as the 3-2 favorite in the Matriarch (gr.1T) at Hollywood Park, when she stumbled after jumping a shadow. Her earnings for 2012 were $515,000.

The year 2013 was an off year for Dayatthespa, earning a "mere" $259,000 from her five starts. Her only two stakes wins were in the listed You Go West Girl at Belmont Park and her second Yaddo for New York–breds at Saratoga. However, she did manage two seconds in the Eatontown at Monmouth Park and the First Lady Stakes (gr.1T) at Keeneland, the latter by a nose to Better Lucky on a soft turf.

Dayatthespa, Javier Castellano up, on his way to winning the 2014 Breeders' Cup Fillies and Mares Turf. *Photograph by Frank Moulton, courtesy of the National Museum of Racing and Hall of Fame.*

After a nine-month layoff, she returned to action on August 2, 2014, with a second in the DeLaRose at Saratoga. She never lost another race the rest of her career. On October 4, she won the First Lady (gr.1T) at her favorite track, Keeneland, at odds of 7-2, with the 5-2 favorite Filimbi in third. She saved the highlight of her career for last on November 1, when she won the 1¼-mile Breeders' Cup Filly and Mare Turf (gr.1T) at Santa Anita in gate-to-wire fashion at odds of 5-1. Finishing second, 1¼ lengths behind, was Stephanie's Kitten, 9-2, and the British star Dank, the 2-1 favorite who had won the 2013 edition of this race, was fourth. That performance by Dayatthespa was enough to be voted that year's Eclipse Award for Filly and Mare Turf. Her earnings for her four starts that year were $1.45 million. Two days after the Breeders' Cup, she was sold for $2.1 million to Stonestreet Farm in Lexington, Kentucky.

CLUSTER OF STARS F. (2009; GREELEY'S GALAXY— BABYURTHEGREATEST, BY HONOUR AND GLORY)

Breeders: Michael McPoland and Sean Finn
Owner: Turtle Bird Stable (Harvey Weinstein)
Trainer: Steve Asmussen
Jockey: Javier Castellano
Career Statistics: 7 starts, 7 wins, $549,600

The filly sprinter Cluster of Stars was unraced at 2 and had one maiden win as a 3-year-old. After winning her first three races in 2013 on the inner dirt track at Aqueduct, including the listed Correction Stakes, on April 13 she won the Distaff Handicap (gr.2) on Aqueduct's main dirt track as the 2-5 favorite. As in all her wins, she went gate to wire. One month later, she ran the best race of her career when she won the Gallant Bloom Stakes (gr.2) at Belmont Park by 5 lengths as the 3-1 third choice. The second-place horse, the 2-1 favorite Dance to Bristol, had won her last seven races, including the Honorable Miss Handicap (gr.2) and the Ballerina (gr.1). The third-place horse, the 5-2 second choice Dance Card, was making her first start of the year after winning the 2012 Gazelle (gr.1). On October 19, Cluster of Stars won her seventh and last race when she took the Iroquois for New York–breds as the 1-5 favorite. On November 11, she returned unsatisfactorily from a workout and was retired.

WILLY BEAMIN G. (2009; SUAVE—BIG TEASE, BY GOLD TOKEN)

Breeder: Patricia S. Purdy
Owners: MeB Racing Stables; James Riccio
Trainers: Dominick Schettino; Richard Dutrow Jr.; William Cesare
Jockey: no main jockey
Career Statistics: 17 starts, 7 wins, 3 seconds, $739,045

After winning a maiden race in four starts as a 2-year-old and finishing ninth in an allowance race for New York–breds to open his 3-year-old season, on March 23 Willy Beamin won a $25,000 claiming race at Aqueduct and was taken by trainer Richard Dutrow Jr. for James Riccio. The claim was

Willy Beamin, Alan Garcia up, warming up prior to the 2012 King's Bishop. *Michele Williams.*

an instant success, as he won his next six races. The first five were for New York–breds, including the Mike Lee and Albany Stakes. Three days after the Albany, he won the King's Bishop Stakes (gr.1) at Saratoga at odds of 11-1. Finishing second, half a length behind, was Fort Loudon at 14-1. Prominent trailers were Currency Swap, the 4-5 favorite who had previously won the 2011 Hopeful (gr.1) and 2012 Amsterdam Stakes at Saratoga, and ninth was the 5-2 second choice Trinniberg, winner of that year's Woody Stephens (gr.2), Bay Shore (gr.3) and Swale (gr.3) Stakes.

After the King's Bishop Stakes, he traveled west to race in the $400,000 Oklahoma Derby at Remmington Park. He finished second, as the 2-1 favorite, ¾ of a length behind the winner, Politically Correct. His trainer for that one race was William Cesare. Returning east, he ended his season by finishing second in the Discovery Handicap and fifth in the Fall Highweight Handicap. His total earnings for the year were $689,225, a great return on a $25,000 investment.

After going winless in three starts in 2013, he was retired to begin training for a new career at New Vocations in Lexington, Kentucky.

The Lumber Guy c. (2009; Grand Slam—Boltono, by Unbridled Song)

Breeder: Stonewall Farm (Barry Schwartz)
Owner: Barry Schwartz
Trainers: Mike Hushion and Neil Drysdale
Jockey: no main jockey
Career Statistics: 13 starts, 4 wins, 2 seconds, 1 third, $790,300

Unraced at two, The Lumber Guy lost no time in breaking his maiden, doing it on January 6, 2012. One month later, he won his first stake, taking the 7-furlong Miracle Wood at Laurel as the 2-5 favorite. On April 12, he tasted defeat for the first time, finishing fifth, 8 lengths behind Gemologist and Alpha in the 9-furlong Wood Memorial (gr.1). On April 12, he cut back in distance to 1 mile, taking the Jerome Stakes (gr.2) as the 2-1 second choice. On May 12, he once again showed his distance limitations by finishing up the track in the 1⅛-mile Peter Pan (gr.2) at Belmont Park. After a four-month layoff, he came back to win the 6-furlong Vosburgh Invitational (gr.1) against older horses.

On November 3, he ran the best race of his career, finishing second in the Breeders' Cup Sprint (gr.1) at Santa Anita at odds of 7-2, half a length behind the 13-1 winner, Trinniberg. Finishing far back in eighth was the 2-1 favorite Amazombie, the previous year's winner. While Hushion returned east, The Lumber Guy stayed in California under the tutelage of Neil Drysdale, and on December 26, he finished sixth in the 7-furlong Malibu (gr.1) as the 4-5 favorite. The winner, Jimmy Creed, had finished ninth in the Breeders' Cup Sprint.

The Lumber Guy returned east to train for his 4-year-old season, but Hushion decided to rest him when he didn't like the way he was training; he never raced again. He was sent to Keane Stud in Armenia, New York.

Weemissfrankie f. (2009; Sunriver—Starinthemeadow, by Meadowlake)

Breeder: Hidden Points Farm (Peter Van Rosebeck)
Owners: Joe Ciagala, Nick Cosato, Rob Dyrdek, Bran Jam Stables (Mike Mellen) and Sharon Alesia
Trainer: Peter Eurton
Jockey: Rafael Bejarano
Career Statistics: 5 starts, 3 wins, 1 third, $559,920

Weemissfrankie (named after the late actor and avid horse player Frank Alesia, whose widow was part of the filly's ownership) was another New York–bred whose home base was in California. She only had five starts in her career, but two were Grade 1 victories. She began by winning her first start, a maiden event at Del Mar, in which she set a new track record of 0:58.1 for the 5-furlong distance. She followed that by winning the 7-furlong Del Mar Debutante (gr.1) on September 3 and the 8½-furlong Oak Leaf (gr.1) one month later at Santa Anita. Her next stop was the Breeders' Cup Juvenile Fillies (gr.1) on November 4 at Churchill Downs. She was the 5-1 third choice, with My Miss Aurelia, winner of the Adirondack (gr.2) and Frizette (gr.1), the favorite at 2-1, and Spinaway (gr.1) winner Grace Hall the second favorite at 7-2. The three fillies finished in that order, with My Miss Aurelia winning by 3 lengths and Grace Hall in second, 6 lengths in front of Weemissfrankie.

After the Breeders' Cup, Weemissfrankie returned to California to compete in the Hollywood Starlet (gr.1) on December 10 as the 9-10 favorite. She finished fourth, 2¾ lengths behind the winner, Killer Graces, but after the race, it was discovered that she had suffered a condylar fracture to her right leg, which ended her career. After her retirement, she was sold to Katsumi Yoshita's Northern Farm in Hokkaido, Japan.

AGAVE KISS F. (2009; LION HEART—SALTY ROMANCE, BY SALT LAKE)

Breeder: Nustar Breeding (Carl Lizza)
Owner: Flying Zee Stables (Carl and Viane Lizza et al.)
Trainer: Rudy Rodriguez
Jockeys: Ryan Curatolo and Ramon Dominguez
Career Statistics: 10 starts, 6 wins, 1 second, 1 third, $339,400

The sprinter Agave Kiss won her two starts as a 2-year-old by 6¼ and 10½ lengths, respectively. She began her 3-year-old season by winning the Ruthless over Aqueduct's inner dirt track by 3½ lengths as the 4-5 favorite. Two months later, she won her fourth straight race when she won the Cicada (gr.3) by 3 lengths as the 1-4 favorite. Five weeks later, she ventured outside her native state, winning the Trevose Stakes at Parx as the 1-2 favorite. On May 18, she stretched her winning streak to six when she won the Miss Preakness Stakes at Pimlico as the 3-5 favorite. All six of her

Agave Kiss, Ramon Dominguez in the irons, warming up prior to the 2012 Prioress. *Michele Williams.*

races were won going gate to wire, and she was the less than even-money favorite in all of them.

The Miss Preakness Stakes would be the last win of her career. After a two-and-a-half-month layoff, she returned to action in New York, tasting defeat for the first time on July 7 at Belmont Park when she finished fifth, 12½ lengths behind the Allen Jerkens trainee Emma's Encore in the listed Victory Ride as the 3-10 favorite. The winner was the longest shot in the six horse field at 39-1. On August 4, Emma's Encore beat Agave Kiss once again in the Prioress Stakes (gr.1) at Saratoga, with the latter finishing a respectable third, 1½ lengths behind. Unfortunately for the bettors, they installed Agave Kiss as the 9-10 favorite, with Emma's Encore only the third favorite at 5-1. The second choice, Judy the Beauty at 3-1, finished second, a neck behind the winner.

Two months later, with much of her respect with the betting public restored by her excellent showing in the Prioress, she lost the Valor Lady on a muddy Belmont track by a neck to Belle of the Hall as the even-money favorite. On October 20, she finished seventh, 14½ lengths behind, in the Iroquois for New York–breds as the 3-2 favorite on another muddy track at Belmont Park. Shortly after the race, she was sold for $250,000 to assume broodmare duties at Gainesway Farm near Lexington, Kentucky, where she had a date pending with major sire Tapit.

Palace c. (2009; City Zip—Receivership, by End Sweep)

Breeder: Peter J. Callahan Revocable Trust
Owners: WinStar Farm; Linda Rice; Antonio Miuccio
Trainers: Bill Mott; Linda Rice
Jockey: Cornelio Velasquez
Career Statistics: 30 starts, 12 wins, 7 seconds, 5 thirds, $1,586,550

Unraced at two, the sprinter Palace did not begin to show his true talents until the end of his 4-year-old season and didn't become a legitimate star until 2014. After losing his first three starts in 2012, he broke his maiden in a $20,000 maiden claiming event on October 6 and was claimed out of that race, going from trainer Bill Mott and WinStar Farm to Linda Rice. After winning two allowance races, Rice sold Palace to Antonio Miuccio, who retained Rice as the colt's trainer.

After the ownership change, Palace spent the next nine months racing in allowances, winning two of five races. On August 23, he won his first stakes race, taking the Chowder's First, followed on October 19 by a win in the Hudson, at odds of 12-1 and 2-1, respectively, both races for New York–breds. In his next start, on November 28, he won the Fall Highweight Handicap (gr.3) at Aqueduct at odds of 5-2. He ended his 4-year-old season by placing sixth in the Gravesend as the 7-10 favorite. His earnings for his breakout season were $424,250.

In 2014, he emerged as one of the best sprinters in the East, with seven of his eight races in graded events, four of them Grade 1s. He began on January 16 by finishing second in the restricted Gold and Roses Stakes, the last time that year he would run in an ungraded stake. One month later, he traveled to Laurel, finishing fourth as the even-money favorite in the General George Handicap (gr.3). After a three-and-a-half-month layoff, he ended his three-race losing streak by taking the 6-furlong True North (gr.2) on June 2 at Belmont Park at odds of 9-1 as the 124-pound highweight.

One month later, he finished second in the Belmont Sprint Championship (gr.3) at odds of 4-1, 6½ lengths behind the 2-1 favorite, Clearly Now. Palace rebounded by winning his first two Grade 1s, the 6-furlong Alfred G. Vanderbilt Handicap at 2-1 and the 7-furlong Forego Handicap, both at Saratoga. In the Forego, he got revenge on the 4-5 favorite, Clearly Now, who finished a distant eighth. Three weeks later, he finished third in

Palace, Cornelio Velasquez up, on the way to winning the 2014 Forego. *Michele Williams.*

the Vosburgh Invitational as the even-money favorite, 1½ lengths behind Private Zone, the 2013 winner of that race. He ended the season on November 1 in the Breeders' Cup Sprint. Although he finished sixth at odds of 7-1, he was only 3 lengths behind the winner, 19-1 Work All Week, and according to the chart, he had a troubled trip: "Palace, three wide between rivals early, was steadied off the heels of Private Zone near the half mile pole, bumped with Bakken around the turn."[40] Palace, a former $20,000 claimer, earned $797,500 from eight starts in 2014.

By 2015, the 6-year-old's best days were behind him. He had only one win in seven starts, that coming in the Hudson Stakes for New York–breds, with seconds in the Fall Highweight Handicap (gr.3) and the Gravesend. He was sold to Spendthrift Farm in Kentucky to begin breeding in the 2016 season.

Unbridled Command c. (2009; Master Command— Unbridled Betty by Unbridled Song)

Breeders: Sequel Thoroughbreds and A. Lakin and Son
Owners: Lewis G. Lakin; Kevin Banford, Colleen Banford and David Bernson
Trainers: Tom Bush; Ed Dunlop; Gary Contessa
Jockey: no main jockey
Career Statistics: 18 starts, 6 wins, 1 second 3 thirds, $515,665

The turf specialist Unbridled Command had an undistinguished career as a 2-year-old and halfway through his 3-year-old season, winning three of six races, all on the turf, and none in stakes races of any kind. After taking a state-bred optional claiming race at Saratoga, his status changed on September 2 when he won the 1⅛-mile Saranac (gr.3T) at Saratoga at odds of 10-1. He continued to impress when, on October 20, he beat New York–breds in the Mohawk by 6 lengths at odds of 5-2. He then traveled west and won the 1¼-mile Hollywood Derby (gr.1T) by 1½ lengths at odds of 7-1. Grandeur, the lukewarm favorite at 7-2 who finished second, later beat older horses in the Hollywood Gold Cup (gr.2T). His four-race winning streak was a successful coda for the season, in which he won $436,000.

During the winter, he was sold to Australians Kevin and Colleen Banford and American David Bernson, who planned to race him in the Royal Ascot in England and the $3 million Cox Plate in Australia, as well as other lucrative events. He would be trained by Englishman Ed Dunlop.

Before he was shipped to England, Unbridled Command was scheduled to race in the Gulfstream Park Turf Handicap (gr.1T) on February 9. The field was the best he had ever faced, headed by the 4-5 favorite Animal Kingdom, winner of the 2011 Kentucky Derby and a close second to Wise Dan in the 2012 Breeder's Cup Mile (gr.1T). The 2-1 second favorite, Point of Entry, had previously won the 2012 Man o' War (gr.1T), Sword Dancer (gr.1T) and Joe Hirsch Turf Classic (gr.1T). Unbridled Command was the third favorite at 7-2, and the bettors correctly gave the other three entrants little chance. Point of Entry won the race by 1¼ lengths, with Animal Kingdom in second, 2¼ lengths ahead of Unbridled Command, the third-place finisher.

The Gulfstream Park Handicap was the last time he would appear in the limelight, as things did not go according to plan in England. He "met with a setback whilst [in England] and was returned to the United States."[41] He raced six times in 2014 on both coasts, finishing out of the money in all of them, and was retired.

ZIVO C. (2009; TRUE DIRECTION—AMERICAN ZIPPER, BY QUIET AMERICAN)

Breeder/Owner: Thomas Coleman
Trainer: Chad Brown
Jockeys: Jose Ortiz and Jose Lezcano
Career Statistics: 19 starts, 9 wins, 3 seconds, 4 thirds, $1,017,300

Unraced at two, it took Zivo three races to break his maiden on June 15, 2012. In his fourth race, on August 22, he finished second to the speedy Willy Beamin in the restricted Albany Stakes at Saratoga. After the Albany, he was out of action for a year to deal with a lower leg problem before returning on August 4, 2013, to finish third in an optional claiming for New York–breds. He raced in three more similar events, with two thirds and a win, followed on November 16 by a second in the restricted Move It Now Stakes. In his last race of the year, on December 14, he won another optional claimer for New York–breds, which would be the start of a six-race winning streak. Four of those races would be New York–bred events—an optional claimer and the Whodam, Kings Point and Commentator Stakes.

Zivo, Jose Lezcano in the irons, warming up prior to the 2014 Woodward. *Michele Williams.*

On July 5, 2014, he broke out of his New York–bred routine in spectacular fashion when he won the 1¼-mile Suburban Handicap (gr.2) at odds of 13-1. Not only did he beat three Grade 1 winners, as well as the 2-1 favorite Romansh, whose two previous races had been a win in the Excelsior Handicap (gr.3) and a second in the Metropolitan Handicap (gr.1), but before the Suburban, he had also never won a race longer than 8½ furlongs.

Two months later, he finished fourth in the 1⅛-mile Woodward Stakes (gr.1) at Saratoga at odds of 3-1, 3 lengths behind the 5-2 second favorite Itsmyluckyday. Zivo's next test was the 1¼-mile Jockey Club Gold Cup (gr.1) at Belmont Park at odds of 4-1. He finished a troubled second, 1¾ lengths behind the 3-1 favorite Tonalist. He lost any chance of winning when a horse ahead of him suddenly bore out to avoid a fallen jockey. Commented Zivo's jockey Jose Lezcano after the race, "I can't believe I ran second. I had to completely stop at the three-eighths pole, and he still came back and finished second."[42]

Zivo's last race of the year was the Breeders' Cup Classic (gr.1) at Santa Anita Park on November 1. He finished eighth at odds of 11-1. The winner, Bayern, and the next five horses after him were all 3-year-olds, and the only older horse to beat Zivo was the seventh-place horse, Cigar Street. Before the race, Steve Haskin noted the lack of talented older horses in the field and thought that Zivo was an "unknown quantity…who can upset the sophomores this year."[43]

Zivo was on the shelf for ten months following the Breeders' Cup, presumably nursing an injury, before he returned to finish fourth in the Evan Shipman for New York–breds. He was retired to stud at Irish Hill Century Farm.

Chapter 5

HORSES BORN 2010–2018

DISCREET MARQ F. (2010; DISCREET CAT—TO MARQUET BY MARQUETRY)

Breeder: Patricia Generazio
Owners: Patricia Generazio; Moyglare Stud Farm Ltd. (Fiona Craig)
Trainers: James Ryerson; Jane Cibelli; Christopher Clement
Jockey: no main jockey
Career Statistics: 24 starts, 8 wins, 5 seconds, 5 thirds, $1,268,072

The front-running turf specialist Discreet Marq raced in New York, Maryland, Florida and California at distances ranging from 5½ furlongs to 9 furlongs during her four-year career. She was trained by James Ryerson and Jane Cibelli through January 1, 2013, and by Christopher Clement for the rest of her career.

She had two wins in five starts in her 2-year-old season, her one stakes win being in the Lie Low at Aqueduct. On May 27, 2013, in her first start with Christopher Clement, she won the $1^1/_{16}$-mile Sands Point (gr.2T) at Aqueduct at odds of 5-2. After taking the restricted Eventail at Belmont, she traveled to California, winning the 1⅛-mile Del Mar Oaks (gr.1T) at odds of 9-2. Returning east, she finished second to Alterite in the 1⅛-mile Garden City (gr.1T) at Belmont Park as the 5-2 favorite. She ended her 3-year-old season by winning the $200,000 Pebbles at Belmont Park and,

Discreet Marq, Irad Ortiz Jr. in the irons, warming up prior to the 2014 Diana. *Michele Williams.*

once again traveling to California, lost the 1-mile Matriarch (gr.1T) by a head bob at odds of 8-1 to Egg Drop at Hollywood Park. Her earnings in 2013 were $657,500.

Although she had an off-year in 2014, winning only the Ticonderoga for New York–breds, she still managed to finish second in the Jenny Wiley (gr.1T) at Keeneland, third in the Diana Stakes (gr.1T) at Saratoga and second to Dayatthespa in the Yaddo, earning $348,000 for her efforts.

After the Ticonderoga, she was sold for $2.4 million to Moyglare Stud Farm Ltd. with the original intention of sending her to Ireland to be a broodmare. It later decided to race her for one more year in the United States, retaining Christopher Clement as her trainer. Although she won her first race of 2015 in the Beaugay (gr.3T) at Belmont, she lost the last three races of her career, finishing third in the Just a Game (gr.1T), fifth in the Yaddo and eleventh in the Ticonderoga.

La Verdad f. (2010; Yes It's True—Noble Fire, by Hook and Ladder)

Breeder: Eklektikos Stable (Mark Vondrasek)
Owners: Eklektikos Stable; Lady Sheila Stable (Sheila Rosenbloom)
Trainer: Linda Rice
Jockey: Jose Ortiz
Career Statistics: 25 starts, 16 wins, 3 seconds, $1,563,200

La Verdad was an Eclipse Award winner whose usual running fashion was going gate to wire. After beginning her career on March 15, 2012, by finishing fourth in a New York–bred maiden special weight, she won six races in a row, from April 7 through January 17, 2014. Before her last race in 2013, she was purchased in a private sale by Lady Sheila Stable, with Linda Rice remaining as her trainer. Her first win of the 2014 season, an optional claiming event, would be the last time in her career she would run in a non-stakes race.

On January 22, 2014, she made her stakes debut, finishing second in the Barbara Fritchie Handicap (gr.2) at Laurel as the 2-1 second choice. She then went on a four-race winning streak, beginning with the Broadway against New York–breds, followed by her first graded stakes win in the Distaff Handicap (gr.2), and two more New York–bred races, the Critical Eye and the Dancin Renee. She was the favorite in all four. She then went on a three-race losing streak, finishing fifth in both the Honorable Miss Handicap (gr.2) and Ballerina Handicap (gr.1) at Saratoga and second by a head in the Gallant Bloom (gr.2) at Belmont. In the latter two, she lost to the brilliant New York–bred Artemis Agrotera. She ended her sophomore season by winning the restricted Iroquois and finishing seventh in the Fall Highweight Handicap, with earnings of $632,400.

La Verdad began her championship 2015 season with five straight wins, including her second Distaff Handicap (gr.2), the Vagrancy Handicap (gr.3), the Honorable Miss Handicap (gr.2) and the Gallant Bloom Handicap (gr.2). Her Honorable Miss win was later disallowed following a positive for clenbuterol. With the exception of one of those races, she went off as the less than even-money favorite. The one exception was the Honorable Miss, when she was 1.30-1 second choice, with that year's reigning female sprinting champion, Judy the Beauty, going off as the .95-1 favorite, finishing 4¾ lengths behind La Verdad in third (moving up to second following the disqualification).

La Verdad's next race was the Breeders' Cup Filly and Mare Sprint (gr.1) at Keeneland, She finished second at odds of 6-1, 1¾ lengths behind the winner, Wavell Avenue, 10-1, whom she had beaten earlier by half a length in the Gallant Bloom. Finishing a non-threatening fourth was the 3-1 favorite Cavorting, who had earlier won the Prioress (gr.2) and Test (gr.1) at Saratoga. La Verdad ended her season with a sixth in the Fall Highweight Handicap (gr.3). She had earnings in 2015 of $722,500.

In the voting for the Eclipse Award for female sprinters, La Verdad edged out Wavell Avenue by eight votes. She raced once more, winning the Interborough Handicap on January 9. Although she was scheduled to run in the Barbara Fritchie (gr.2) at Laurel, it was decided to retire her while she was ahead.

London Bridge c. (2010; Arch—Kindness Girl, by Indian Ridge)

Breeder: Patricia S. Purdy
Owners: Eastwind Racing (Mikael Magnusson and Robert Trussell) and Martha
*   Trussell; Waratah Thoroughbreds (Paul Fudge)*
Trainers: Mikael Magnusson; Joanne Hughes
Jockey: Mike Smith, for his only start in America (no main jockey in Europe)
Career Statistics: 9 starts, 4 wins, 1 third, $307,969

London Bridge was as cosmopolitan as a Thoroughbred can get. He was bred in New York, had an English mare for a dam, an Irish horse for his dam's sire, was owned by an Australian, raced most of his career in England and France and won his only stake in the United States. He was winless in his only start in 2012, after which he was owned for the rest of his short career by Waratah Thoroughbreds. He ran his first six starts as a 3-year-old in England, his next race in France in August, with four wins. He was then shipped to his native country, and on November 1, 2013, he won the 1¾-mile Breeders' Cup Marathon (gr.2) at Santa Anita, the only 3-year-old in the race. He went off at odds of 9-1, and it was his only start on the dirt. He was the first New York–bred to win a Breeders' Cup race, and Hughes was the third female trainer, and the first female European trainer, to do so. He never raced again and was shipped to be a stallion at Carrington Park Stud in the Southern Highlands, Australia.

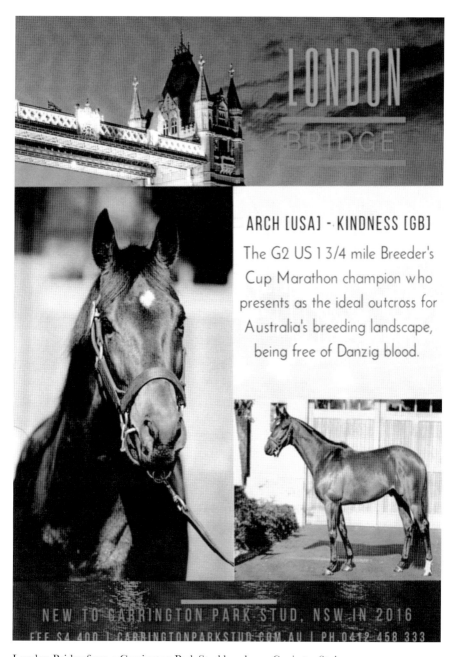

London Bridge from a Carrington Park Stud brochure. *Carrington Stud.*

Effinex c. (2011; Mineshaft—What a Pear, by D Dubai)

Breeder: Dr. Russell S. Cohen
Owner: Tri-Bone Stable (Bernice Cohen)
Trainers: David Smith and James Jerkens
Jockeys: Mike Smith and Junior Alvarado
Career Statistics: 28 starts, 9 wins, 3 seconds, 4 thirds, $3,312,950

According to a popular story, Effinex got his name because his owner had been involved in a bitter divorce case. However, Dr. Cohen (who could be called Effinex's quasi-owner since he bred Effinex for his mother, and Effinex was the only horse in Tri-Bone's stable), although amused by the rumor, claimed that his horse's name came from the German word that means "integrity and efficiency."[44]

Unraced at two, Effinex had a profitable but uneventful career as a 3-year-old. After he finished sixth in an optional claimer for New York–breds, Jimmy Jerkens took over the training duties from David Smith. Three races later, on October 18, he won the $300,000 Empire Classic for New York–breds at odds of 17-1. He ended the year with fourths in the Hawthorne Gold Cup (gr.2) and restricted Alex M. Robb, giving him final earnings of $345,850, respectable but insignificant to what he would earn his last two years of racing.

After beginning 2015 by winning an optional claiming race on March 27, he won his first graded stakes, taking the 1¼-mile Excelsior (gr.3) at Aqueduct at odds of 6-1. His next start, on June 6, was a disaster, being pulled up the 1½-mile Brooklyn Handicap at Belmont Park at odds of 3-1 after going wide the first two turns. A rider change to Junior Alvarado paid immediate dividends on July 4 when he won the 1¼-mile Suburban Handicap (gr.2) at odds of 6-1. Finishing behind him was the 2-1 favorite and 2014 Belmont Stakes (gr.1) winner Tonalist, who was conceding six pounds to Effinex.

After a two-month layoff, Effinex returned to action in the 1⅛-mile Woodward Stakes (gr.1), finishing fourth, 6½ lengths behind the winner, Liam's Map, who would later that year win the Breeders' Cup Dirt Mile (gr.1). On October 3, continuing his battles against the best handicap horses in the country, he finished third in the 1¼-mile Jockey Club Gold Cup (gr.1) on a sloppy Belmont Park track. He was 11½ lengths behind old foe Tonalist, whom he had beaten earlier in the Suburban but now raced at equal weights of 126 pounds.

Effinex, Mike Smith in the irons, during the stretch drive at the 2016 Whitney. *Michele Williams.*

Three weeks later, he raced in the 1¼-mile Breeders' Cup Classic (gr.1) at Keeneland, finishing second at odds of 33-1. The winner was the 7-5 favorite American Pharoah, that year's Triple Crown winner. Behind Effinex were Honor Code (third), winner of the Metropolitan Mile (gr.1) and Whitney Handicap (gr.1), and Tonalist (fifth), who, like Effinex and Honor Code, carried 126 pounds. Three weeks later, on November 27, Effinex closed out his year by winning his first and only Grade 1, taking the Clark Handicap at Churchill Downs as the 5-2 favorite. Finishing second was the 2014 winner of the Clark, Hopportunity. His earnings for 2015 were a lofty $1,767,100. He also finished fourth in the voting for the Eclipse Award for older males behind Honor Code, Liam's Map and Tonalist.

In 2016, Effinex won the Oaklawn Handicap (gr.2) and his second Suburban Handicap (gr.2), with Samraat finishing second for a $56.50 New York–bred exacta. He also finished second to Melatonin in the Santa Anita Handicap (gr.1) as the 3-2 favorite and second in the Jockey Club Gold Cup (gr.1) as the even-money favorite, with Hoppertunity the winner. His earnings for 2016 were $1.2 million. He retired after the 2016 season, taking up stallion duties at Questroyal North. In late September 2018, he relocated to McMahon of Saratoga, where on the night of October 18 he died suddenly in his stall of a ruptured pulmonary artery. Dr. Cohen explained what the horse meant to him: "It is not a business to me. This is a passion….He is the kind of horse every owner should have at least once in their life. He filled a huge void in my life."[45]

HAVEYOUGONEAWAY F. (2011; CONGRATS—ONE WISE COWGIRL, BY WISEMAN'S FERRY)

Breeders: Andy Breadwell and Susan Breadwell
Owners: Champion Racing Stable (Ricky C. Cundrift); Gary Barber and Sequel Racing
Trainers: Allen Milligan; Thomas Morley
Jockey: Jareth Loveberry
Career Statistics: 27 starts, 11 wins, 4 seconds, 6 thirds, $907,425

The sprinter Haveyougoneaway, unraced at two, spent the first two and a half years of her career running in the south and southwest. After breaking her maiden in her second race in 2014, she finished eighth in the Fantasy (gr.3) at Oaklawn Park, the last time she would run in a graded race until July 27, 2016. Under her original connections, she won the 2015 Flashy Lady at Remmington Park and the 2015 and 2016 American Beauty at Oaklawn Park. After finishing second in the Carousel at Oaklawn Park on April 14, 2016, she changed venues and trainers, moving to her native state, with Tom Morley taking over the training duties.

After finishing second in the Critical Eye for New York–bred at muddy Belmont Park on May 16, she won the Dancin Renee, also for New York–breds. On July 27, she took the 6-furlong Honorable Miss (gr.2) at Saratoga at odds of 7-2. Losing by a neck was the 3-2 favorite Paulassilverlining, who had previously won the Humana Distaff (g.1) and Madison (gr.1) Stakes. She followed that with the biggest win of her career, taking the 7-furlong Ballerina Stakes (gr.1) at Saratoga at odds of 10-1. Finishing third was the even-money favorite, Carina Mia, who had previously won the Acorn (gr.1). Finishing fifth was Paulassilverlining. She ended her career by finishing seventh in the Breeders' Cup Fillies and Mares Sprint (gr.1). Her earnings for 2016 were $655,000.

Haveyougoneaway. John Velasquez up, prior to the 2016 Ballerina. *Michele Williams.*

Artemis Agrotera f. (2011; Roman Ruler—Indy Glory, by A.P. Indy)

Breeders/Owners: Chester Broman and Mary Broman
Trainer: Mike Hushion
Jockey: no main jockey
Career Statistics: 10 starts, 5 wins, $943,800

The filly sprinter Artemis Agrotera showed her ability in her first start as a 2-year-old, breaking her maiden by 11¾ lengths on August 18 at Saratoga. One and a half months later, she continued to impress when she won the one-mile Frizette Stakes (gr.1) at 4-1, with the future star Stopshoppingmaria finishing 4 lengths back in third. On November 13, she ran in the 1 1¹/₁₆-mile Breeders' Cup Juvenile, showing possible distance limitations when she finished fifth, 11¼ lengths behind Rio Antonia, the winner by disqualification. That rival had finished fifth in Artemis Agrotera's Frizette victory. She finished the year with earnings of $402,000 for her three starts.

She began 2014 on June 7 with another disappointing race, finishing eighth in the one-mile Acorn Stakes (gr.1). On July 23, she won a New York state-bred optional claimer by 10½ lengths, and one month later, she took the 7-furlong Ballerina Stake (gr.1) at Saratoga by 6½ lengths at odds of 4-1. Her time of 1:21.89 was faster than what the 3-year-old colts ran in the King's Bishop Stakes (gr.1) one race earlier.[46] On September 20, she won her third straight race, taking the 6½-furlong Gallant Bloom Handicap (gr.2) by a head as the 2-5 favorite despite being the only 3-year-old in the race. The chart maker was unusually extravagant in his praise: "Artemis Agrotera…was forced by [Willet] to take the five path for entrance into the stretch, kicked into her best stride after getting straightened away, charged home with an amazing display of determination and speed to wrest away the decision in the last jump."[47] Casey Laughter was also impressed: "This

Artemis Agrotera, Rajiv Maragh up, on her way to an easy win in the 2014 Ballerina. *Michele Williams.*

filly's performance was nothing short of spectacular.…Artemis Agrotera is likely the best female sprinter in the country."[48]

Her last race of the season was another bad performance at her least favorite track, Santa Anita in the Breeders' Cup Filly and Mare Sprint (gr.1). Despite being the 9-2 third choice, the best she could do was a no-excuse seventh, 12 lengths behind the winner and 3-1 favorite, Judy the Beauty. Although her bad performance might have cost her an Eclipse Award, she still managed to win $541,800 for the season.

On December 12, it was announced that Artemis Agrotera was being retired to be a broodmare. However, those plans changed; in September, Hushion said that his filly had some sensational works and that she would train up to the Breeders' Cup Filly and Mare Sprint (gr.1) on October 15 at Keeneland. It would be her first race since her last Breeders' Cup at Santa Anita. Artemis Agrotera was never better than eighth in the race and finished last of the fourteen horses. She was now ready to become a broodmare.

Samraat c. (2011; Noble Causeway—Little Indian Girl, by Indian Charlie)

Breeder/Owner: My Meadowview Farm (Leonard Riggio)
Trainer: Rick Violette
Jockey: Jose Ortiz
Career Statistics: 15 starts, 5 wins, 3 seconds, 1 third, $1,050,400

Samraat's career was like a meteor that shot up in the air, reached an apex and then crashed to earth. He won all three of his starts as a 2-year-old, including the Damon Runyon for New York–breds. He began his sophomore season by winning the Withers (gr.3) and Gotham (gr.3). The Gotham, his fifth win in a row, would be the last victory of his career. On April 5, he finished second in the Wood Memorial (gr.1) at odds of 3-1, 3½ lengths behind 9-1 Wicked Strong.

The Wood was followed by a respectable fifth in the Kentucky Derby at odds of 16-1, won by California Chrome. His next race was a sixth in the Belmont Stakes, 4 lengths behind the winner, Tonalist. He missed the rest of the year recovering from a stress fracture to his right shin sustained during a workout and didn't return until he ran in an optional claiming race on July 7, 2015, at Belmont, finishing second. During that race, he reinjured his shin and was out until April 8, 2016, when he finished fourth in an optional claiming race. He raced five more times in 2016, his best being seconds in the Westchester Handicap (gr.3) and Suburban Handicap (gr.2). In the latter, the winner was Effinex, resulting in a $56.50 New York–bred exacta.

He raced once more, on July 2, 2017, finishing sixth in the Saginaw for New York–breds to Diversify, and was retired.

Wired Bryan c. (2011; Stormy Atlantic—Red Melody, by Runaway Groom)

Breeder/Owner: Antsu Farm
Trainer: Michael Dilger
Jockeys: Sean Bridgmohan and John Velazquez
Career Statistics: 6 starts, 4 wins, 1 second, $537,474

Wired Bryan had a brief but lucrative career. After breaking his maiden at first asking, on July 21, 2013, he won the Sanford Stakes (gr.3) at Saratoga by 5½ lengths at odds of 7-1. On August 11, he finished second in the Saratoga Special (gr.2), a nose behind the winner, Corfu. Three weeks later, he threw his only clunker, finishing sixth in the Hopeful Stakes (gr.1) at Saratoga, 12 lengths behind the winner, Strong Mandate. He ended the year by winning

Wired Bryan, Shaun Bridgmohan in the irons, closing in on a 5½-length win in the 2013 Sanford. *Michele Williams.*

the $237,000 New York Breeders' Futurity by 7 lengths at Finger Lakes and $150,000 Bertram F. Bongard at Belmont, both restricted to New York–breds and both at less than even money. He was done for the season; his future plans were to train for possible participation in the 2014 Triple Crown events, but he never raced again, probably because of an injury. In February 2015, he was sold for $30,000 to be a stallion in Uruguay.

Disco Partner c. (2012; Disco Dancer—Lulu's Number, by Numerous)

Breeder/Owner: Patricia Generazio
Trainers: James Ryerson; Christopher Clement
Jockeys: Junior Alvarado and Irad Ortiz Jr.
Career Statistics: 28 starts, 11 wins, 5 seconds, 6 thirds, $1,487,560

The turf sprinter Disco Partner was slow to mature, not winning his first graded race until halfway through his 4-year-old season. He did earn $188,311 in his first two years, most of that money coming from New York–bred events. In 2016, his earnings jumped to $178,500 from only five starts, his best race being a loss by less than a nose to Pure Sensation in the Jaipur (gr.3T) at Belmont Park. Both the Jaipur and Pure Sensation would be important factors in Disco Partner's later career. He also won his first stake that year, taking the Troy Handicap at Saratoga, followed by a fourth, 1¾ lengths behind Pure Sensation in the $150,000 Belmont Turf Sprint Invitational.

After a six-and-a-half-month layoff, he began 2017 with a new trainer, switching from Jim Ryerson to Christopher Clement, and a new jockey in Irad Ortiz Jr. Showing no rust, he won the Elusive Quality at Belmont Park as the 5-2 favorite. His next race, on June 17, marked his debut as a serious sprinter, taking the Jaipur Stakes (gr.3T) while setting a new world record of 1:05.3 for the 6-furlong distance on the turf. On July 15, he won the longest race of his career, taking the one-mile Forbidden Apple at Belmont Park as the even-money favorite. His three-race winning streak ended on August 12 in the one-mile Fourstardave Handicap (gr.1T), finishing fourth as the 3-2 favorite on a yielding Saratoga main turf course. He got back on the winning track on October 10 when he won the Belmont Turf Sprint Invitational at odds of 3-10. He ended his 5-year-old season with a third in the Breeders' Cup Turf Sprint (gr.1T) at odds of 5-1, half a length behind the 30-1 winner, Stormy Liberal. Finishing fifth was his nemesis and now stablemate, Pure Sensation, and finishing tenth was the 9-10 favorite Lady Aurelia. Disco Partner's earnings for 2017 amounted to $547,000.

He began his 6-year-old season with a third in the Shakertown (gr.2T) on April 7, followed two months later with his second Jaipur (gr.3T) win. After a fifth in the Forbidden Apple and a third in the Troy Handicap (gr.3T) at Saratoga, he won for the last time in his career, taking his second Belmont Turf Sprint Invitational. On November 3, he finished third in the Breeders' Cup Turf Sprint (gr.1T) to Stormy Liberal for the second year in a row, 7½ lengths behind the winner. On November 24, he ended his season with a second to stablemate White Flag in the Aqueduct Turf Sprint Championship, giving him earnings of $467,250.

After a winless 2018 in five starts, he was retired to assume stallion duty at Rockridge Stud in Hudson, New York.

UPSTART c. (2012; FLATTER—PARTY SILKS, BY TOUCH GOLD)

Breeder: Mrs. Gerald A. Nielsen
Owners: Ralph M. Evans and WinStar Farm
Trainer: Rick Violette
Jockey: Irad Ortiz Jr.
Career Statistics: 15 starts, 4 wins, 3 seconds, 4 thirds, $1,732,780

Even as a 2-year-old, Upstart was considered a coming star of his generation. He broke his maiden at first asking at Saratoga on August 11, and nine days later, he won his first stakes race, taking the Funny Cide for New York–breds. After a seven-week layoff, he returned to action in the one-mile Champagne Stakes (gr.1) at Belmont Park, finishing second at 7-2 to Daredevil. One month later, he assured himself of the reputation as a horse to be respected in the 2015 season when he finished third as the 6-1 third favorite in the Breeders' Cup Juvenile to 14-1 Texas Red. The 6-5 favorite Carpe Diem was second, a nose ahead of Upstart. The 5-2 second choice, Daredevil, finished eleventh and last. Upstart's earnings from his four starts were $463,800.

He began his 2015 season with a win in the 1¹⁄₁₆-mile Holy Bull Stake (gr.2) at Gulfstream Park as the 2-1 second choice. The 3-2 favorite Frosted was in second, 5½ lengths behind Upstart. Finishing fifth was Keen Ice, 15-1, who would later defeat Triple Crown winner American Pharoah (and Upstart) in the Travers Stakes (gr.1). In its account of the race, *Blood-Horse* called Upstart "a prime contender on the Triple Crown trail."[49] Although he finished first in his next race, the 1¹/₁₆-mile Fountain of Youth Stakes (gr.2) on February 21 as the 9-10 favorite, he was disqualified to second for bearing out into Itsaknockout in deep stretch, with Itsaknockout declared the winner.

The Fountain of Youth would be the last time he would cross the finish line first in 2015. In the 1⅛-mile Florida Derby (gr.1), he finished second as the even-money favorite, 2½ lengths behind Materiality. His next start, the Kentucky Derby, was a disaster, checking in sixteenth and last at odds of 15-1, with the 2-1 favorite American Pharoah winning the first leg of his Triple Crown procession. On August, he had the misfortune of facing American Pharoah again in the 1⅛-mile Haskell Invitational (gr.1) at Monmouth Park, finishing 5½ lengths behind the Triple Crown winner and 3 lengths behind second-place finisher, Keen Ice. In his next race, the 1¼-mile Travers Stakes (gr.1), he once again finished behind American Pharoah, but ahead of both

Upstart, Irad Ortiz Jr. in the irons, warming up before the last race of his career in the 2016 Whitney. *Michele Williams.*

of them was Keen Ice in a startling upset. After a fifth in the Pennsylvania Derby (gr.2), he was given the rest of the year off. Despite his disappointing finish, he still managed to win $786,480 in 2015.

Upstart began 2016 on a winning note, taking the 1 1/6-mile Razorback Handicap (gr.3) at Oaklawn Park. It would be the last win of his career. He finished fourth in the Oaklawn Handicap (gr.2) to fellow New York–bred Effinex; third in the Metropolitan Handicap (gr.1), 15 lengths behind the winner, Frosted; and third in his swan song, the Whitney Stakes (gr.1), 2½ lengths behind Frosted. He won $482,500 in 2016.

At first glance, it would appear that Upstart went into decline after his successful campaign at Gulfstream Park. However, his breeding might have been the main reason for his later lack of success. In an article in the *Blood-Horse* following the Fountain of Youth, Avalyn Hunter wrote, "Although Upstart has a better pedigree for getting a distance than many of his contemporaries, there is reason to think he might be better suited to intermediate distances. The reasons start with Flatter….Flatter has only two winners at the graded or listed levels at nine furlongs." She continued to question Upstart's dam, Party Silks, concluding that she did not have the bloodlines to supply "that [missing] stamina."[50] After that piece was written, it should be noted, Upstart never won a race beyond 8½ furlongs, and that is only partially attributed to the equine buzz saw named American Pharoah.

After his retirement, he took up stud duties at Airdrie Stud near Midway, Kentucky.

Bar of Gold f. (2012; Medaglia D'Oro—Khancord Kid, by Lemon Drop Kid)

Breeders/Owners: Chester Broman and Mary Broman
Trainer: John Kimmel
Jockeys: Junior Alvarado and Jose Ortiz
Career Statistics: 25 starts, 7 wins, 6 seconds, 4 thirds, $1,551,000

Before the last race of her career, the sprinter Bar of Gold was already a millionaire despite never having won a graded stakes. Although she was basically a sprinter on the dirt, she was versatile enough to have won some 1¹/₁₆-mile races, races in the slop and a win, one second and one third in

Bar of Gold, Jose Lezcano up, in the stretch in the 2017 Ballerina. *Michele Williams.*

four races on the turf. Before her surprising win in the Breeders' Cup, she had success in graded stakes races, finishing second in the 2015 Test Stakes (gr.1), Prioress Stakes (gr.2) and Raven Run Stake (gr.2) and the 2017 Ruffian Stakes (gr.2) and Presque Isle Masters (gr.2). Bar of Gold was entered in the 2017 Breeders' Cup Filly and Mare Sprint (gr.1) at Del Mar with some reluctance on the part of Kimmel. In the race leading up to the Breeders' Cup, the 1⅛-mile Spinster (gr.1) on a sloppy artificial dirt track at Keeneland, she had finished sixth as the 3-2 favorite. That race mystified Kimmel, but after his mare returned to New York, she had several excellent workouts with regular jockey Irad Ortiz Jr. in the irons. Kimmel decided to ship Bar of Gold and Ortiz to California, and to the surprise of everyone, she rallied from sixteenth to win by a nose at odds of 66-1. Left in her wake were the even-money favorite Unique Bella (seventh), winner of four straight graded stakes going into the race; the 6-1 second choice, Skye Diamonds, winner of a Grade 2 and a Grade 3; and the 7-1 third choice, Finley'sLuckyCharm (ninth), winner of two Grade 3's and a Grade 2. Finishing ninth at odds of 18-1 was Bar of Gold's stablemate and nemesis Highway Star. Her $135.40 payoff for a $2.00 bet was the largest in the race's history, and it was Kimmel's first Breeders' Cup win.

If you're going to cap your career with your first graded stakes win, you might as well do it in a Breeders' Cup. The $550,000 she won in that race pushed her 2017 earnings to $822,000.

International Star c. (2012; Fusaichi Pegasus— Parlez, by French Deputy)

Breeders: Katharine M. Voss and Robert T. Manfusco
Owners: Kenneth Ramsey and Sarah Ramsey
Trainer: Michael Maker
Jockey: Miguel Mena
Career Statistics: 18 starts, 6 wins, 4 seconds, 1 third, $1,247,629

Although International Star ran his first three starts in New York, he spent the rest of his career outside the Empire State. After winning a maiden race on the turf and finishing second in the Rockville Centre on the dirt, both New York–bred events at Belmont Park, on August 8 he finished second in the With Anticipation Stakes (gr.2) at Saratoga. It was his last race in New York State. On October 5, he finished first in the Grey Stakes (gr.3) on Woodbine's artificial surface, followed by a ninth in the Breeders' Cup Juvenile Turf (gr.1T) at Santa Anita. After that race, Ramsey told his trainer "not to get enamored with the turf, because that's not why I bought him."[51] International Star spent the last fourteen races of his career on the dirt.

His first three races of his sophomore year were the apex of his career, winning all the Kentucky Derby preps at the Fair Grounds in New Orleans. He began the year on January 17 by winning the Le Comte (gr.3) at 9-1, 2½ lengths ahead of War Story. On February 15, he won the Risen Star (gr.2) at 7-2, with War Story once again finishing second. On March 28, he completed his Fair Ground triple by taking the Louisiana Derby (gr.2) by a neck over Stanford, with War Story in third. Prominent among the also-rans in the last two races was Keen Ice, who later in the year defeated American Pharoah in the Travers (gr.1). The Kentucky Derby was in Ramsey's sights, but on the day of the Derby, International Star was scratched due to heat in his left front foot. Several days later, that diagnosis was changed to a hairline knee fracture, which put him on the shelf for the next seven months. He returned to end his season with a fourth in the Zia Park Derby, finishing the 2015 with earnings of $818,400 from only four starts.

The last two years of International Star's career were anticlimactic, his only win coming in the 2016 Louisiana Stakes at his favorite track, Fair Grounds. He also placed in the 2016 Fair Grounds Handicap (gr.2), the New Orleans Handicap (gr.2), both to Mike Maker-trained S'Marvelous, and the 2017 Mineshaft Handicap (gr.3), all at Fair Grounds. He ended his career on May 17, 2017, with a third in the Alysheba (gr.3) at Churchill Downs.

In 2020, he was sold to Havas Porta Pia Stud Farm near Santiago, Chile.

HIGHWAY STAR F. (2013; GIROLANO—STOLEN STAR, BY CAT THIEF)

Breeders/Owners: Chester Broman and Mary Broman
Trainer: Rodrigo A. Ubillo
Jockey: Angel Arroyo
Career Statistics: 23 starts, 10 wins, 5 seconds, 2 thirds, $1,326,813

Unraced at two, the sprinter Highway Star spent most of her 3-year-old season making a good living racing against New York–breds, culminating on November 13 when she won her first stakes, taking the $125,000 New York Stallion Series by 3½ lengths as the even-money favorite. In her next race, she ended her 3-year-old season by winning the Go for Wand (gr.3) at 7-1. Her earnings for 2016 were $369,000.

She began 2017 by finishing fourth in the 1-mile, 70-yard Ladies Handicap. It would be the last bad race she would run until November. After what turned out to be a beneficial layoff, she dropped back to 7 furlongs, taking the Distaff Handicap (gr.3) at Aqueduct at odds of 5-1. On May 13, she won the one-mile Ruffian Stakes (gr.2) on a sloppy Belmont track, with the even-money favorite and stablemate Bar of Gold finishing half a length back in second. That finish resulted in a $29.40 New York–bred exacta.

On June 10, she stepped up in class, finishing third in the 8½-furlong Ogden Phipps Stakes (gr.1) at odds of 9-1, 3½ lengths behind the 2015 and eventual 2016 filly champion Songbird, who was the logical 3-10 favorite. Highway Star had now graduated from a good New York–bred to the upper range of filly sprinters on the East Coast. Her reputation was further enhanced when, on August 26, she lost by a head at 5-1 to By the

Highway Star, Angel Arroyo up, prior to the 2017 Ballerina. *Michele Williams.*

Moon in the 7-furlong Ballerina Stakes (gr.1) at Saratoga, while the 2-1 favorite Paulassilverlining languished in fifth. One month later, she won the Gallant Bloom Handicap (gr.2) at 2-1, with the even-money favorite Carina Mia a neck behind in second.

Highway Star's next scheduled race was the Breeders' Cup Filly and Mare Sprint (gr.1) at Del Mar on November 4. Before they left for California, her handlers decided as an afterthought to include her 5-year-old stablemate Bar of Gold, considered to be the lesser of the two, to run in the same race. As related earlier, the Bromans won the race, but not with Highway Star, who went off at 18-1. The winner was the unheralded (and, for the most part, unbet) Bar of Gold, who paid a whopping $135.40. Highway Star ended her season on December 2 by finishing second in the Go for Wand Stakes (gr.3). Despite her poor showing in the Breeders' Cup, she still managed to win $640,000 in 2017.

Although she didn't win any graded stakes in 2018, her last year, she still managed to earn $317,818. Prominent among her races were seconds in the Ruffian Stakes (gr.2) and the Bed o' Roses Invitational (gr.3).

Diversify g. (2013; Bellamy Road—Rule One, by Street Cry)

Breeders: Fred W. Hertrich III and John D. Fielding
Owners: Lauren Evans and Ralph M. Evans
Trainers: Rick Violette; Jonathan Thomas
Jockeys: Jose Ortiz and Irad Ortiz Jr.
Career Statistics: 16 starts, 10 wins, 2 seconds, $1,989,425

Unraced at 2, Diversify had only two races at 3, breaking his maiden in his inaugural race. After beginning his 4-year-old season with seconds in an allowance and the restricted Commentator Stakes, on July 2 he started on a four-race winning streak, beginning with the Saginaw and Evan Shipman Stakes for New York–breds. He then ascended into the company of elite handicap horses with a win in the 10-furlong Jockey Club Gold Cup (gr.1). Finishing a length behind was the 3-2 favorite Keen Ice. Violette stated after the Jockey Club, "He's always been a nice horse, but he's certainly jumped into the major leagues today."[52]

He lost his next race, the Clark Handicap (gr.1) at Churchill Downs, although Irad Ortiz Jr. claimed that he did not like the track. After Diversify showed some soreness following the race, Violette decided to give him some time to recover. His earnings for the year amounted to $690,825.

After he began his 2018 season on April 21 by finishing last as the heavy favorite in the 9-furlong, three-turn Charles Town Classic (gr.2), he began a three-race winning streak with a victory against New York–breds in the Commentator, followed on July 7 by a dominating 3½-length win in the Suburban Handicap (gr.2) at Belmont Park. The bettors sent him off at 6-1, but he demolished a field that included such standouts as Tapit, Hoppertunity and War Story. Turf writer Sarah Mace characterized the race as a "tour de force performance," and Violette considered it better than his win in the 2011 Jockey Club Gold Cup.

After a one-month layoff, Diversify returned to action to face fellow New York–bred Mind Your Biscuits and six others in the Whitney Stakes (gr.1) at Saratoga. After the track turned sloppy by a torrential downpour that delayed the race for forty-five minutes, the 8-5 favorite Diversify won by 3½ lengths, with Mind Your Biscuits completing a New York–bred $10.30 exacta.

On September 29, Diversify finished fifth in the Jockey Club Gold Cup (gr.1). That result, in addition to trainer Rick Violette's worsening condition from his long bout with cancer, persuaded the gelding's co-owners Ralph

Diversify, Irad Ortiz up, on his way to a win in the 2018 Whitney. *Michele Williams.*

Evans and his daughter, Lauren, to avoid that year's Breeders' Cup Classic. After Violette's death on October 21, Diversify was sent to Florida with new trainer Jonathan Thomas to begin training for either the Pegasus (gr.1) or Dubai World Cup (gr.1). Neither race materialized for Diversify, and he returned to New York to get ready for his 2019 season. When he sustained a suspensory injury during a workout, the Evans team decided to retire their star and send him to Old Friends in Kentucky.

VOODOO SONG C. (2014; ENGLISH CHANNEL—MYSTIC CHANT, BY UNBRIDLED SONG)

Breeder: Stonewall Farm (Barry Schwartz)
Owner: Barry Schwartz
Trainers: Mike Hushion; Linda Rice; Richard Mandela
Jockey: Jose Lezcano
Career Statistics: 20 starts, 6 wins, 2 seconds, 1 third, $883,435

The front-running turf specialist Voodoo Song had a fair record as a 2-year-old, breaking his maiden on the turf, with two close losses on the dirt. After beginning his 3-year-old season by losing two New York–bred races on the dirt by 10½ and 16½ lengths, two changes happened that changed his career: Mike Hushion was replaced by Linda Rice, and he was switched to the turf.

On July 17, in his first start under Linda Rice, he won an open company 8½-furlong $40,000 claiming race on the turf by 5½ lengths at what was to be his favorite track, Saratoga. His hooves never touched dirt in a race again. After two more wins against New York–breds at Saratoga, he continued his rapid ascent by winning the 1⅛-mile Saranac Stakes (gr.3T) by a nose at odds of 6-1. Although he was probably reluctant to leave Saratoga, on September 30 he broke his four-race winning streak by finishing second in the Commonwealth Derby (gr.3T) at Laurel as the 3-5 favorite. On October 8, he ended his 3-year-old season by finishing fifth as the 9-10 favorite in the Hawthorne Derby. The 2017 earnings for the former $40,000 claimer came to $355,085, most of which came from Saratoga.

He began his 4-year-old season by winning two of three races at Belmont, including the Forbidden Apple against New York–breds. His next start was the apex of his career, winning the one-mile Fourstardave Handicap (gr.1T) at, where else, Saratoga, at odds of 9-2. Finishing sixth and last was the 2-1 favorite Heart to Heart, who had previously won the 2018 Gulfstream Park

Voodoo Song, Jose Lezcano, warming up prior to the 2017 Saranac. *Michele Williams.*

Handicap (gr.1) and Makers 46 Mile (gr.1). It was fitting that the greatest race of his career was named for another horse who had a fondness for Saratoga.

The Fourstardave would be the end of his status as among the elite of the country's turf runners. His next race brought his five-race winning streak at Saratoga to an end when he finished fifth in the Bernard Baruch Handicap (gr.1T). Linda Rice was still thinking of the Breeders' Cup, but that plan was scrapped when he finished twelfth and last in the Shadwell Turf Mile at Keeneland. His 2018 earnings came to $480,350.

He was winless in 2019, with two seconds against New York–breds, in five starts. Later in the year, he changed trainers and coasts, going to Richard Mandella and California. In his only start in 2020, he finished sixth in the San Simeone (gr.3T) at Santa Anita, and in September he was retired to assume stud duties.

Mind Your Biscuits c. (2013; Posse—Jazzmane, by Toccet)

Breeder: Jumping Jack Racing (Samantha Will Baccori)
Owners: J Stables, Head of Plains Partners, Shadai Farms, Chad Summers and
    M. Scott Summers
Trainers: Roy Falcone Jr.; Chad Summers
Jockey: Joel Rosario
Career Statistics: 25 starts, 8 wins, 10 seconds, 3 thirds, $4,279,566

Mind Your Biscuits was an exceptional sprinter for most of his career and later had some success at 9 furlongs. As of 2020, he holds the record for the most career earnings for New York–breds.

Although it took him five races to break his maiden, it only took him four more to win his first stakes, taking the Amsterdam (gr.2) on July 30, 2016, at Saratoga at odds of 3-1. In his next race, on August 27, he ran into a monster, finishing fifth in the King's Bishop Stakes (gr.1). The winner was the Bob Baffert–trained 3-1 favorite Defrong, who would go on to be that year's champion sprinter. After finishing second to Noholdingback Bear in the 6-furlong Gallant Bob (gr.3) at Parx on November 5, he lost to Defrong again in the Breeders' Cup Sprint, finishing third, 1¼ lengths behind the winner at odds of 15-1. On December 26, he ended his three-race losing streak by taking the 7-furlong Malibu Stakes (gr.1) at Santa Anita at odds of 7-2, with Defrong sitting out the race. His earnings for the year were $740,400.

Mind Your Biscuits, Joel Rosario up, heading to the finish in the 2017 Dubai Golden Shaheen. *Dubai Racing Club.*

Mind Your Biscuits, Joel Rosario up, winning the 2018 Dubai Golden Shaheen, with XY Jet second and Roy H. third. *Dubai Racing Club.*

After the Malibu, Summers replaced Falcone with himself as Mind Your Biscuits' trainer. His colt began the 2017 season with a loss by a neck to Unified in the Gulfstream Sprint (gr.3) as the 9-10 favorite. On March 25, he caught the international racing world's attention when he won the 1,200 meters (about 6½ furlongs) $2 million Dubai Golden Shaheen at Meydan Racecourse, winning by 3 lengths despite starting from the fourteen hole. After returning to the United States and a three-and-a-half-month layoff, he found the winners' circle again when he took the Belmont Sprint (gr.2) as the even-money favorite. However, his heroics for 2017 were over. He finished sixth in the Forego Handicap (gr.1) at Saratoga to his nemesis Defrong; third in the Breeders' Cup Sprint (gr.1) to Roy H.; and second, 5½ lengths behind Sharp Azteca, in the Cigar Mile Handicap (gr.1). Nevertheless, his earnings for only six starts in 2017 were $1,713,800.

After beginning his 2018 season with a second in an optional claiming race, on March 31 he won his second Dubai Golden Shaheen, with American sprint stars XY Jet second and that year's eventual sprint champion Roy H. third. Two and a half months later, he finished second in the 1-mile Metropolitan Handicap (gr.1), second in the 1⅛-mile Whitney Stakes (gr.1) to fellow New York–bred Diversify and first in the Lukas Classic (gr.3) at Churchill Downs. After finishing eleventh in the Breeders' Cup Classic, Summers planned one more start before his colt's retirement in either the Cigar Mile or Clark Handicap; however, after a dull workout, Shadhai Farm took over full ownership, and he was shipped to Hokkaido, Japan, to assume stud duties. His earnings for 2018 were a tidy $1,770,400, once again with only six starts.

Audible c. (2015: Into Mischief—Blue Devil, by Gilded Time)

Breeder: Oak Bluff Stable
Owners: China Horse Club; Head of Plains Racing; Starlight Racing; WinStar Farm
Trainer: Todd Pletcher
Jockey: Flavier Prat
Career Statistics: 10 starts, 5 wins, 1 second, 2 thirds, $2,130,500

Audible had a brief ten-race career but was arguably the second-best male horse of his generation. After losing the first race of his career, he ended his 2-year-old season by breaking his maiden followed by an allowance win.

He began 2018 by extending his winning streak to three by taking the 1^{1}/16-mile Holy Bull Stakes (gr.2) at Gulfstream Park, followed two months later by the most important win in his career, the 1^{1}/8-mile Florida Derby (gr.1) as the 9-5 favorite. Finishing fourth was 7-2 second favorite Catholic Boy, who later in the season took the Travers (gr.1) at Saratoga. On May 5, he finished third in the Kentucky Derby as the 7-1 fourth favorite, 4^{1}/4 lengths behind the winner, Justify, the 5-2 favorite. The track turned up sloppy, and as often happens in a twenty-horse field, Audible had a rough trip.

Pletcher decided to skip the Preakness to concentrate on the 1^{1}/2-mile Belmont Stakes three weeks later, a decision that was changed later with much controversy. Justify (who continued on his Triple Crown journey by taking the Preakness) and Audible had the same owners, and when Pletcher scratched his horse from the Belmont Stakes, it caused a chorus of turf writers to howl that Audible was scratched because Justify would be worth many millions of dollars if he won the Triple Crown, much more than if Audible won the Belmont. The latter outcome was more than a remote possibility considering Audible's impressive effort in the Kentucky Derby. Pletcher, while acknowledging the controversy, argued that he scratched Audible because his workouts indicated that he was not in top form going into such an important and demanding race.

Justify won the Belmont and was immediately retired to await his lucrative career as a stud. Audible, on the other hand, did not return to racing for six months, lending some credence that Pletcher's explanation was the truth. On November 3, he won the 7-furlong Cherokee Run at Churchill Downs, the last win of his career. On December 15, he finished a disappointing second as the 1-5 favorite to 25-1 Sir Anthony in the Harlan's Holiday Stakes on a sloppy Gulfstream Park track. His earnings for 2018 were $1,141,120.

Audible only raced twice in 2019 before retiring, finishing fifth in both races. However, it was a prosperous season for him, with each race netting him $360,000. On January 5, he ran fifth in the Pegasus World Cup (gr.1) at Gulfstream Park, won by City of Light, and on March 5 he ran fifth in the Dubai World Cup (gr.1), 3^{1}/4 lengths behind the winner, November Snow.

After the Dubai World Cup, he was sent to WinStar Farm to be at stud at a fee of $25,000. Justify's fee at Coolmore Stud was $150,000.

NOTES

Introduction

1. When the legislature passes legislation and forwards it to the governor, his office collects solicited and unsolicited memoranda sent to the governor discussing what the legislation intends to do and why it should be approved or vetoed. If the governor approves, the legislation and the memoranda are put into a Governor's Bill Jacket. If the legislation is vetoed, the material is put into a Veto Jacket. Eventually, the bill and veto jackets are sent to the New York State Library. Often this is the only official source of legislative intent in New York State, although reports of executive, legislative or governors' commissions also are important sources of legislative intent.
2. Bill Jacket, L. 1994, chap. 282, 5.
3. Ibid., 8.
4. Ibid., 14.

Chapter 1

5. Kent Hollingsworth, "Home State's Upstate Upstart," *Blood-Horse*, August 8, 1981, 4,680.
6. Andy Beyer, "Fio Rito Wins Whitney Over Vaunted Field," *Washington Post* archives, August 2, 1981.

7. William H. Rudy, "The Futurity on Ice," *Blood-Horse*, September 8, 1981, 5,688.

8. Zamarelli, Don, "An Open United Nations,"*Blood-Horse*, August 7, 1982, 5,369.

9. Steven Crist, "Man o' War Won by Naskra's Breeze," *New York Times*, October 4, 1982, C13.

10. William H. Rudy, "Again, a Joy," *Blood-Horse*, June 12, 1982, 3,890.

11. Steve Crist, "Cupecoy's Joy Wins the Mother Goose," *New York Times*, June 5, 1982, 17.

Chapter 2

12. Russ Harris, "Flattering Performance," *Blood-Horse*, October 19, 1985, 7,362.

13. Dede Biles, "A Growing Threshold," *Blood-Horse*, June 23, 1984, 4,276.

14. Steven Crist, "Sky High," *Blood-Horse*, July 30.1994, 3,565–66.

15. Bill Finley, "Superstar at Saratoga," *Blood-Horse*, August 20, 1994, 3,866.

16. Joe Agrella, "The Wins of Chicago," *Blood-Horse*, September 5, 1987, 5,306.

17. Neil Campbell, "Ballindaggin's Six-Figure Win," *Blood-Horse*, September 17, 1988, 5,325.

18. Mike Veitch, "Goodbye to a Champion," *New York Thoroughbred*, 1990.

19. Mike Veitch, "Fourstars Allstar Was One of the Greats," March 18, 2005, www.drf.com.

20. Steven Crist, "Ready to Rumble," *Blood-Horse*, August 29, 1992, 3,788.

21. Steven Crist, "Thunder Rolls Again," *Blood-Horse*, August 13, 1994, 3,786.

22. *Blood-Horse*, "Breeders' Cup Distaff IX," November 7, 1992, 5,056.

Chapter 3

23. *Bloodstock in the Bluegrass*, "Broodmare of the Week: Lottsa Talc," May 16, 2012, https://fmitchell07.wordpress.com/2012/05/16/broodmare-of-the-week-lottsa-talc.

24. Marty McGee, "Timarida Makes Statement vs. Top Turf Fillies," *1996 Graded Stakes Yearbook*, 321.

25. *Blood-Horse*, "Incurable Optimist," December 5, 1998, 7,202.

26. Steve Haskin, "Critical Odds," *Blood-Horse*, September 16, 2006, 5,531.

27. Steve Haskin, "It Had to be You," *Blood-Horse*, August 3, 2002, 4,226.

Chapter 4

28. Steve Haskin, "Cide Show," *Blood-Horse*, May 10, 2003, 2,636.

29. Steve Haskin, "Last Laugh," *Blood-Horse*, June 4, 2003, 3,238.

30. Steve Haskin, "Passionate Cide," *Blood-Horse*, October 9, 2004, 5,433.

31. Jeff Johnson, "On the Improve," *Blood-Horse*, April 29, 2006, 2,536.

32. *Blood-Horse*, "Fleet Indian," April 1, 2006, 2,001.

33. *Blood-Horse*, "Emirates Airline Distaff Division," November 11, 2006, 6,429.

34. Paul Volponi, "Speak Up," *Blood-Horse*, August 13, 2005, 4,515.

35. Bill Finley, "Horse Racing: Tough as Well as Fast, Read the Footnotes Wins," *New York Times*, February 15, 2004 (Archives).

36. David Grening, "Read the Footnotes Back," Daily Racing Form, November 25, 2004, www.drf.com.

37. *Blood-Horse*, "Tough Timber," www.bloodhorse.com/horse-racing/articles/139700.

38. *2011 American Racing Manual*, 446.

39. Brisnet, "Bustin Stones Remains Unbeaten in General George," February 19, 2008, http//brcdn.brisnet.com/content/2008/02.

40. *2015 American Racing Manual*, 405.

41. E-mail from Ed Dunlop to Allan Carter, January 17, 2019.

42. Claire Crosby, "Tonalist Captures Jockey Club Gold Cup," *Blood-Horse*, September 23, 2014, 3/13, www.bloodhorse.com/horse-racing/articles/111688.

43. Steve Haskin, "BC Classic: How weak Are the Older Horses?," *Blood-Horse*, October 21, 2014, 3/13, www.bloodhorse.com/horse-racing/articles/111304.

Chapter 5

44. Ryan Martin and Derren Rogers, "Stephen Foster Favorite Effinex Continue [*sic*] Breeder's Joyous Ride," Churchill Downs, June 17, 2016, www.churchilldowns.com/racing-wagering/news.

45. Eric Mitchell, "Effinex Dies Suddenly from Ruptured Pulmonary Artery," *Blood-Horse*, October 19, 2017, 2/11, www.bloodhorse.com/horse-racing/articles/224203.

46. Sarah Mace, "Broman Homebred Artemis Agrotera All Alone at the Wire in Grade 1 Ballerina," New York Breeders, August 23, 2014, https://www.nytbreeders.org/news/2014/08/23/artemis-agrotera-ballerina.

47. *2015 American Racing Manual*, 363.

48. Casey Laughter, "Get to Know: Artemis Agrotera Primed for Breeders. Cup Filly and Mare Sprint," Lady and the Track, September 22, 2014, 1/3, www.ladyandthetrack.com/news/9697.

49. *Blood-Horse*, "Options Abound for Holy Bull Winner Upstart," January 25, 2015, 1/5, www.bloodhorse.com/horse-racing/articles/109492.

50. Avelyn Hunter, "Pegigree Analysis: Upstart," *Blood-Horse*, March 20, 2015, 219, www.bloodhorse.com/horse-racing/articles/108700.

51. Lenny Shulman, "Ramsey Hopes for Shining Star," *Blood-Horse*, April 30, 2015, 3/7, www.bloodhorse.com/horse-racing/articles/107705.

52. Sarah Mace, "Diversify Dazzles in Grade 2 Suburban," New York Breeders, July 7, 2018, 1/3, www.nybreeders.org/news/2018/07/07.

SOURCES

American Racing Manual. Published annually since 1897 by the *Daily Racing Form*, this is a must for anyone writing about horse racing. Includes statistics, graded stakes charts, graded stakes histories, racetrack directories and breeding information. Beginning with the 2020 edition (covering the year 2019), it's available in digitized format only.

Blood-Horse Magazine. Published weekly and indexed at the end of the year. Also available online at www.bloodhorse.com/horse-racing/articles.

Daily Racing Form. The Keeneland Library and the University of Kentucky are collaborating on a project to digitize the entire collection of *Daily Racing Forms* in the Keeneland Library's collection. At present, the project is concentrating on the 1930–50 period, but some entries go back earlier. To access the collection, go to https//drf/uky/edu.

Graded Stakes Yearbook. Published 1997–99 when the *American Racing Manual* temporarily ceased publication. Contains information on every graded stakes held in a given year.

New York Breeder. Published monthly by the New York Thoroughbred Breeders Inc. Also available online at www.nybreeders.org.

New York Times (1851–2011) by ProQuest, available in many public libraries. Subscribers to the *New York Times* also have access to its archives.

INDEX

ABOUT THE AUTHOR

Allan Carter, a native of Glens Falls, New York, graduated from Harpur College (now Binghamton University) with a degree in general literature. Following his graduation, he served four years in the U.S. Army as a Russian linguist, learning that language at the Army Language School. After his discharge, he got his master's in library science and spent his next thirty years as a law librarian at the New York State Library. During his tenure at the state library, he authored many publications, including *Public Library Law in New York State* and *The New York State Constitution: Sources of Legislative Intent*. In 2003, he retired from the state library and took the position of historian at the National Museum of Racing and Hall of Fame in Saratoga Springs, New York, retiring in 2019. He has authored two books on horse racing: *150 Years of Racing in Saratoga: Little-Known Stories and Facts from America's Most Historic Racing City* (coauthored with Mike Kane) and *From American Eclipse to Silent Screen: An Early History of New York–Breds*. He resides in Saratoga Springs with his wife, Paula; their dog, Goody; and their cat, Daisy.

Visit us at
www.historypress.com
···